*To Rich!
You can!
Bless you,
Athena*

A GUIDE TO CHRISTIAN SELF-PUBLISHING

YOU CAN
Do It!

WINEPRESS PUBLISHING

REVISED AND EXPANDED

ISBN 1-883893-82-8

Published by:
WinePress Publishing
PO Box 1406
Mukilteo, WA 98275

Unless otherwise noted, Scripture quotations are from the New King James Version of the Holy Bible. Copyright © 1979, 1980, 1982. Used by permission of Thomas Nelson, Inc. Scripture versions marked NLT are taken from the New Living Translation of the Bible.

To the many Christian writers scattered across the country who have—through their questions, concerns, and stories—inspired me to write this book.

Publish his glorious deeds among the nations.
Tell everyone about the amazing things he does.

—Psalm 96:3, NLT

CONTENTS

INTRODUCTION

I LOOKED FRANTICALLY AROUND the plush lobby of the Sheraton Inn Atlanta. The billboard listed many events, but the Christian writers' conference at which I was supposed to be speaking was not one of them.

"All things work together for good" came quickly to my mind. I dismissed that thought impatiently and thought, "Oh sure, God . . . here I am, stranded!" The nightmare of an overfull calendar colliding with reality had come true. I had written the dates for the conference incorrectly in my Daytimer and was now in the right place at the wrong time. I could feel a lump rising in my throat. I had worked so hard to get everything done so I could be away from the WinePress office for four days. Now I was confronted with the fact that I was in a strange hotel, away from my husband and family, with nothing to do and a nonrefundable plane ticket that forced me to stay over Saturday night. The front desk clerk was nice enough to give me the "airline rate" for my room. When I finally got up there, I fell to my knees.

"Oh, Jesus! Why am I here? How could this have happened? What is going on?"

Ever so gently, that still, small voice whispered into my heart, "You've been asking me for time to write, haven't you?"

The light came on . . . fireworks went off . . . the choir started singing "Glory, Glory, Hallelujah!" That's it! I had spent my whole flight to Atlanta scribbling an outline for the book you are holding in your hand. Above the quiltwork patches of Midwestern farms, I had fine-tuned the outline and had discussed it with God.

"Lord, when am I ever going to have time to write this book? I know I need to, and I know You want me to—but Lord, when?" I didn't get an answer, but I continued writing down ideas for the chapters.

Christian writers' conference directors had been after me for the previous six months to put into print the concepts that my husband and I had learned firsthand in our Christian publishing business and that I taught in my classes. There has been a need for information about self-publishing specifically geared to the Christian market, and many felt that God was going to use me to fill that need.

Within hours I had arranged for a computer and printer to be delivered to my Atlanta hotel room, along with a carafe of hot coffee. Two long, grueling days (and more coffee) later, I emerged from room 310, disk in hand—mission accomplished! Well, at least the first draft of the mission.

God, in His infinite mercy, arranged my circumstances to give me both the time to write the book and the energy to complete it. It was a miracle out of misery. My prayer is that through this book many more miracles will come and many believers will be helped to get their work into print.

Since the first edition of this book was printed, I've watched the Christian publishing industry continue to focus on celebrities and cut back on titles from new authors. And while it was disturbing to read the *World* magazine article on Christian publishing (July 12/19, 1997), it was a sobering confirmation of all that's been happening.

Not long after that article came out I spent some quality time with a well-known author. After twenty years in the industry she finally came to the conclusion that she can't make a living in Christian writing. This prolific writer had received reports from friends and relatives complaining that they couldn't find her books in Christian bookstores. Frustrated and disillusioned, she felt like quitting. Getting the illusive contract with a big publisher is not all it's cracked up to be.

The good news? Such changes in the publishing industry only make self-publishing a much more viable option. WinePress Publishing is blessed by the Lord to be smack dab in the middle of this cutting-edge trend. In fact, that frustrated author is now working for us.

I've added some great new material to this revised and expanded edition of *You Can Do It!* including how to raise the money to fund your project and some great tips on getting the most out of the media. It is my prayer that this information will bless you and enable you to finish the race the Lord has given you to run.

WHY SELF-PUBLISH?

Hᴀs ᴛʜᴇ Lᴏʀᴅ given you a message? Yes? Then why haven't you published it yet? I can almost hear your answer: "I can't find a publisher interested in my book. I keep getting rejection slips." Could it also be that you're not quite sure how to go about it and are afraid of being taken advantage of?

Recently I attended a reunion for Christian Leaders, Authors & Speakers Services (CLASS) that was held during the annual Christian Booksellers Association (CBA) convention. As one of the senior editors for Thomas Nelson Publishing gave her session, I was overwhelmed with how obvious it became that the celebrities were the only ones who would get any attention at all from Thomas Nelson Publishers. She shared that it came down to dollars and cents: If they weren't absolutely sure that they could move 25,000 hardcover copies of a book in the first year, they weren't interested.

If we are going to have realistic expectations, then we ought to take a close look at the Christian publishing industry, the trends, and the real state of affairs. For publishing companies there are basically two ways of doing business. The first is to publish a multitude of titles with the expectation of decent sales for all; the other is to publish fewer titles with high sales volumes for each one. The trend that most Christian publishing companies are following is the second one—fewer titles and higher sales volume—which means "big name" authors. Right there the majority of us are excluded!

At the Mt. Hermon Christian Writers' Conference, I taught a class on self-publishing and one on promoting and marketing your book. After the class I had the opportunity to take in some of the other sessions, so I sat in on one by an editorial representative from a major Christian publishing house. He told how they receive 2,000 unsolicited manuscripts per month and publish only 12 to 17 new titles per year. He went on to explain that in order to be one of their authors you "have to bring something to the table." That list includes:

1. A cutting-edge topic that is unique but still falls into their publishing niche
2. A Ph.D. or some other certified training that makes you an authority in your area
3. Strong communication skills and/or the ability to speak in front of large crowds
4. An established speaking or mail-order ministry that would purchase (in order to sell at your speaking engagements) at least 2,000 copies a year

That certainly rules out many Christian writers. However, just because you may not fit into the narrow criteria of a major publishing house doesn't mean the message God has given you shouldn't be in print. But again, we must be realistic. We need to take a look at the cold, hard facts in Christian publishing today and see what our chances are of selling works to a major Christian publisher, whether as a first-time author or as a self-published success.

The October 16, 1995 issue of *Publisher's Weekly* contains an article entitled "Downsizing Hits Thomas Nelson," in which Byron Williamson, head of the recently formed Nelson/Word Publishing Group, is quoted: "The changes are being made to accommodate a planned reduction in title output. In recent years, Nelson/Word published close to 400 titles annually, but . . . this figure will be cut to about 200 titles by fiscal 1997."[1] This signaled only the beginning of major cutbacks in the industry.

The Writers Information Network printed the following excerpt from a rejection letter penned by the editorial vice president of a major Christian publisher.

> [Our company] has instituted a planned reduction in our title output for the next year. This means we are not accepting any additional projects for the next several months. This is unfortunate, for I do find your project intriguing and the sample material is quite well done! Possibly it could work very well for us. But, as things stand for us at the moment, we are passing on many things we might have gladly published before.[2]

During the Pacific Northwest Book Fair, I met Jay Heinlein who was, at the time, a director of sales for Word Publishing. I let him know about WinePress Publishing and how we help people self-publish affordably (and professionally). Heinlein noted, "We receive as many as 3,000 manuscripts per year and only print approximately 150. Many of those wonderful efforts find other publishers, but sadly many never find a home."

In an early edition of our WinePress newsletter we had an opportunity to interview Bruce Zabel, literary agent for the Curtis Bruce Agency. Bruce had worked sixteen years in the publishing field before becoming an agent. He has worked for InterVarsity Press, Goodnews Publishers, Lion Publishing, and the Right Group. At the time of our interview he was representing several productive and notable authors, such as Mark Littleton, Angela Elwell Hunt, and David and Karen Mains. His comments about the Christian publishing industry were frank and sobering. The interview went like this:

> **Q**: What are some current statistics regarding the book publishing industry?
>
> **A**: Typically there are approximately 1,500 to 2,000 new Christian books published each year. Thomas Nelson, one

of the largest Christian publishers, does approximately 200 to 300 new titles each year. At the other end, some of the smaller organizations will do five to ten books, so you can see there is quite a spread. The book sales figures for all [combined] Christian publishing houses is 800 million to 1 billion dollars annually.

Q: How many manuscripts does the average publisher receive in a year?

A: The big publishers get in the neighborhood of 5,000 to 10,000 *unsolicited* manuscripts per year. However, it is incredibly rare for an unsolicited manuscript to ever get published.

Q: What are some of the factors that make it so difficult?

A: There are tons of books and ideas submitted every day—some solicited and some not. Needless to say, more are submitted than ever get published. The main problem I see is that far more people are writing today than ever, and the number of books being published is not increasing to keep up with what is written. One of the growing practices and trends is for the publishers to use agents, like myself, to do their screening for them. I get a thousand to two thousand ideas or proposals yearly and I reject 99 percent of those, . . . and then of the 1 percent I keep and submit to the publishers, only a fraction get serious consideration. Some publishers *do* look at unsolicited manuscripts still; but it is becoming more and more rare. Most won't even talk to a writer unless he or she has an agent, and writers generally don't pick an agent—the agent picks them!

Q: So what do you see as the major changes or trends in the Christian publishing industry?

A: I think the major trend [now leveling off] is fiction. However, some publishers are now re-evaluating their interest and thoughts on fiction, and I see it slowing down quite a bit in the near future. Another critical change to look at is the cost of publishing a book. As we speak, here in the spring of 1995, the price of paper has been going up for about 18 months now. Consequently, most publishers are looking closer at the number of books they publish, which makes it even tougher for an unknown writer to get a contract. The number of books getting published also seems to be decreasing.

Q: How does the Christian retail bookstore fit into all these trends and changes?

A: This is only an intuitive comment. I'm not sure if there have been any studies done on it, but Christian bookstores are not increasing the amount of space devoted to books. So this, of course, presents another problem. There's no new space being set aside for books, and any free space or shelf space is being given over to gift items, art, and music. In other words, book space is decreasing and gift item space is increasing. One thing I do know: The competition for shelf space is incredibly fierce in the Christian bookstores.

Q: In your opinion, is an unknown author likely to be picked up and contracted by a royalty publisher like Zondervan, Thomas Nelson, or Multnomah?

A: It does happen from time to time, but to answer your question . . . it's not likely. It is rare because the bigger publishers, and you can't fault them for this, would rather go with someone who has a proven track record and is a proven seller and a proven commodity mover. So for an unknown author to be published by them is rare. It does happen, but not too often.

Q: What is your opinion of self-publishing?

A: Well, I actually have a handful of clients who have done some self-publishing. They have also subsequently gone on to publish with a traditional publisher. I would say this: If you have a forum from which to sell your books, or a "built-in" market, so to speak, it could work out for you. That's the first thing. You just can't publish books and not have a way to get them to people who might want them. Second, if you have the time and inclination to invest in selling and marketing your books, either as a part-time or a full-time business, then it could be a very viable way to go. It could result in a successful venture for you.

Q: Do you have any concluding comments that may help or encourage our readers?

A: Yes. I have known some self-publishing ventures that have been very successful. They have gone to an organization like WinePress that helped them edit, stylize, typeset, and print their book. In this way they have gotten it into presentable form [which is crucial]. Then they turned around and sold those books and made a good profit. They were able to see lifelong dreams come true. Their message was in print and selling. These folks had a forum and a market, and I'll reiterate: This is a critical factor in deciding whether to self-publish or not.[3]

In order to intensify your reality check, pick up a copy of the *Christian Writers' Market Guide* by Sally Stuart. You'll see all the various Christian publishers listed in alphabetical order. You will notice in the information that each company includes the percentage of first-time authors they publish. Sadly, the percentage numbers are almost always very low.

As I speak at the various Christian writers' conferences, I am sometimes concerned with the message that often comes across from some of the better-known authors. I've heard comments like, "Don't quit; if I can do it, you can do it. I just signed a three-book contract with a major publisher before ever actually writing the manuscripts. . . . I work in my sweats, in the comfort of my own home, set my own hours. I am a full-time Christian writer. Now, it took me fifteen years to get to this place. If I can do it, every one of you can too."

The unreal expectations fanned into flame by such comments concern me. I agree that you should not quit. If God has given you the gift or burden for writing, you should do all you can to perfect your craft, and you should be persistent. But whether or not your name will be in lights as a well-known author just because you keep at it for fifteen years is still highly unlikely. I know that authors who make these remarks mean well and are trying to encourage the conferees, but I feel these remarks are unrealistic.

I received this e-mail message from one of the attendees of that specific conference.

Dear Athena: Thank you for bringing a realistic view of both the difficulties and the possibilities of self-publishing. You certainly erased all our vainglorious imaginations and lofty ideas of seeing our names in lights. You brought us back to earth, and at the same time you gave us hope!

I must admit I was saddened to see that all I've been noticing in the Christian publishing industry has been confirmed. At the 1997 Christian Booksellers Association International Convention (CBA), a very disturbing article was the talk of the show. "Whatever Happened to Christian Publishing?" reiterates the dreadful state of affairs in our industry. The author has given me permission to reprint the article in its entirety.

Visitors to the Christian Booksellers Association convention in Atlanta, July 14–17, will walk into the ultimate trade show. The latest T-shirts, plaques, CDs, and software will all be on display. Celebrity authors will sign autographs. Bookstore owners will be feted at hospitality suites. Publishing insiders will schmooze and make deals.

Last year's convention attracted 13,663 attendees, including 2,801 store representatives and 419 exhibitors from what has become, according to published reports, a $3 billion industry. But such dramatic material success is not without its price. Today the largest Christian publishers are owned by secular corporations or have shares held by Wall Street investors. As ministries turn into big businesses, theological integrity can easily give way to marketing considerations. The attendant [cutthroat] competition, coupled with theological looseness, can lead to promotion of a new, watered-down, pop Christianity.

The trend concerns many Christians who work in book publishing. Although one source was willing to be named in this article, all the others spoke only under conditions of confidentiality, because they legitimately fear a kind of excommunication from the tightly knit industry. Information for this story was gathered from trade publications, published articles, and dozens of interviews, conversations, and e-mail correspondence with editors, writers, and other industry insiders.

⌒—

Christian publishing in America has a long and distinguished history, but the contemporary story begins five years ago, with two buyout offers.

Thomas Nelson Publishers generated one of the buyouts, purchasing Word for $72 million in cash, according to *Business Wire*. Nelson/Word is now the largest player in the Christian publishing industry. Though the two companies retain their separate names and catalogs, many of their operations have been combined. This year, Word is moving its corporate headquarters from Dallas to Thomas Nelson's offices in Nashville. The merged companies make up a single corporate entity, owned by stockholders.

Zondervan Publishing House employees tried the other buyout. Their company had been purchased in 1988 by HarperCollins, a publishing segment of Rupert Murdoch's empire. (The Australian billionaire also owns the Fox television network and has just purchased the Family Channel.) Four years later, a management-led group of employees tried to buy the company back. James Buick, then president of Zondervan, told The *Grand Rapids Press* that the group's purpose was to "return the direction and control of the company into the Christian community." But according to the *Grand Rapids Business Journal*, the effort failed and HarperCollins solidified its control.

Opinions differ on whether that is a problem. In today's Byzantine world of corporate conglomerates, a company can theoretically have absentee landlords while retaining considerable independence. Secular ownership poses special problems, though, for Christian publishers. Church-related companies can ask questions about an employee's faith, but publicly held or secular operations are not allowed to discriminate on the basis of religion. Christian ministries are often concerned for evangelism and doctrinal fidelity, but secular corporations are motivated mainly by the bottom line.

According to Len Goss, a former Zondervan editor currently with Broadman & Holman, HarperCollins and Mr. Murdoch at first adopted a hands-off policy. The religious commitment of its employees was delicately taken into account, and the company was allowed to do as it had been doing. But after a few years, he said, the corporate owners did interfere.

Mr. Goss told *World* that HarperCollins handed down a dictate that Zondervan publish more big sellers and cut down on the rest. As a result, the academic line on which Mr. Goss worked was scrapped, and the focus shifted to mass-market titles, to books that could meet sales thresholds by appealing to the broadest possible audience. Spokesmen for Zondervan did not return *World*'s calls seeking comment.

Thomas Nelson and Zondervan now are the Big Two of the Christian bookselling industry, an industry that is going through some introspection after a highly successful first half of the decade. Between 1991 and 1994 sales of religious books jumped from 36.7 million to 70.5 million, according to *Christianity Today*, a 92 percent boost that moved religious books from a 5 to [a] 7 percent market share.

The lucrative growth of the religious market pleased investors, but it added to the pressure to focus on big sellers. This pressure was accentuated by other changes in the religious marketplace that forced even the smaller publishers to adapt to the ways of big business.

Christian bookstores have long been the main retail outlet for the industry. The same consolidation that was taking place with the publishing companies was taking place with Christian bookstores. Family-owned and ministry-related local businesses were giving way to chain stores and retail franchises. One advantage of such franchises is that they can buy books en masse and supply stores with sharply discounted product. The priority, however, is on stocking fewer titles, often only those with big sales and high turnover, according to a John Armstrong article in *Viewpoint: A Look at Reformation & Revival in Our Time*.

Here's another obstacle publishers face: In a typical Christian bookstore today, books now make up only 28 percent of sales, according to *Publisher's Weekly*. T-shirts, CDs, videos, inspirational plaques, greeting cards, and knickknacks take up two-thirds of the shelf space, leaving little room for the display of books that are not bestsellers.

Big wholesalers that supply the bookstores are also contributing to the new market considerations. Retailing insiders note that many booksellers take seriously the task of selecting the books they stock, but it is far easier—and often more profitable—to take advantage of their suppliers' offer to ship only those projected to be the top-selling titles. This sets up a self-fulfilling prophecy, as books that might well have turned out to be strong sellers never make it to the shelves, while the books given special favor by the publishers and wholesalers are the only ones available for customers to buy.

Authors too are getting swept up into the new religious market. Though writers are of course essential to the publishing process, they often complain of being neglected, exploited, or—in an industry highly dependent on ghostwriters—invisible. But those Christian authors who do sell well, like their secular counterparts, increasingly use agents to negotiate mega-deals.

Ever since Chuck Swindoll used an agent in 1989 to negotiate a [forty-five]-title, [ten]-year contract with Word, the most popular Christian writers have been offering their services to the highest bidder with the help of agents. *Publisher's Weekly* last year recounted how an agent scored a five-year, [eleven]-book contract for historical novelists Brock and Bodie Thoene in a bidding war finally won by Nelson for a reported $3.5 million.

Though such arrangements are clearly good for superstar writers, use of agents changes the relationship between author and publisher into a purely financial one as opposed to the personal and collaborative relationships that sometimes occurred in the past. Another consequence, lamented in writers' conferences, is that new, less-established authors find it harder to get published, as many editors grow dependent on agents and refuse even to look at unsolicited manuscripts.

(Most such manuscripts, publishers note, are not worth their reading. But what happens to the rare exception? Even a [bestseller]—[like] *This Present Darkness*, Frank Peretti's first supernatural thriller—can occasionally be fetched out of what book companies call the "slush pile.")

Most Christian publishing companies, including the Big Two, began as family-owned ventures closely tied to a ministry or to a church body. Many of the smaller to medium-sized publishers continue in that manner and are organized as nonprofit or church-related organizations. But today, through their own policy decisions or out of necessity, they are having to function in the tough world of big [business].

Though many publishing companies and editors are still working out of a strong Christian commitment and are publishing valuable Christian books, competing in today's religious marketplace poses special challenges and temptations.

Surely the free-market economy is a good thing. America's prosperity and freedoms are tied to marketplace competition and disciplines. But while consumerism, the profit motive, and survival of the fittest are good for the realm of economics, they should not rule theology. Jesus, who drove the salesmen out of the temple, warned about the impossibility of serving both God and money. The prophets strenuously denounced religious leaders who told the people pleasant words from their own minds rather than the unsettling truths of the Word of God.

The apostle Paul could have been describing today's religious marketplace: "For the time will come when men will not put up with sound doctrine. Instead, to suit their own desires, they will gather around them a great number of teachers to say what their itching ears want to hear" (2 Tim. 4:3). A free-market economy, catering to consumer desires, gives us convenient supermarkets and shopping malls. But a marketing approach to religion requires "suiting desires" that because of the Fall are innately evasive of God. Religious consumerism involves "scratching ears" by telling the customers only what they want to hear, instead of the Word of God they need to hear.

The Christian marketplace thus follows the lead of the world's pop culture. A common saying in the industry is[:] Whenever a trend emerges in the secular arena, wait six months and a Christianized version will appear in the religious bookstores. Romances, horror novels, management books, and other popular genres that are essentially written according to easy-to-follow formulas rather than original insights, all have their counterparts in Christian bookstores.

Our culture's obsession with physical beauty gives rise to Christian diet plans and Christian exercise videos. Even when it comes to religion, Christian publishing often follows trends rather than leads, as in the rash of books on angels and near-death experiences inspired by New Age books on the same subjects.

One phenomenon of America's pop culture is celebrity worship. Books by sports stars, entertainers, or other icons of the pop culture—a significant number of which are ghost-written—have become big sellers for Christian publishers. While testimonies of conversion have long been staples of evangelicalism, sometimes the mere fact of celebrity seems to justify publishing an individual's life story.

One editor offered the example of the autobiography of hamburger mogul Dave Thomas, founder of Wendy's. Though the book, [copublished] by Zondervan and HarperCollins, is generically inspirational and has a first-rate title—*Well Done*—it has almost no explicit Christian content.

Some celebrity authors—the Billy Grahams and the Chuck Swindolls—have a strong track record in ministry and teaching. Others, however, are motivational speakers or positive-thinking gurus whose works may be uplifting but are at best only remotely connected to the biblical worldview. Such writers are entitled to their say and may be worth reading, but the question, again, is why are they published by presses that claim to be evangelical?

Self-help is another popular category for evangelical publishers, despite the irony that "self help" would seem to be the opposite of the historic evangelical emphasis on the grace of God. Many of these titles—such as Thomas Nelson's *Don't Let Jerks Get the Best of You*—are little more than pop psychology, with the standard secular bromides of self-esteem and assertiveness training. Others approach the Bible itself as a self-help manual.

Here again, the publishers are merely following the market instead of attempting to teach. Polls have shown that many Americans are interested in the Bible insofar as it can give "practical principles for successful living." Christian publishers, instead of finding ways to show that the Word of God has the power to save, sometimes domesticate it into a rule book for a contented, prosperous, middle-class lifestyle. Thomas Nelson offers titles such as *The Management Methods of Jesus* and *The People Skills of Jesus: Ancient Wisdom for Modern Business.*

The desire for market share, the yearning for acceptance by mainstream American culture, and the overweening goal of many Christian publishers to cross over into the bigger secular market, sometimes result in even bigger doctrinal compromises. Word's *Searching for God in America*, based on a PBS series that gave Islam and Buddhism equal time with Christianity, portrays the different faiths as equally valid paths to God.

Some smaller publishers resist the pressures of commercialism and continue to publish theological books— but some of them nevertheless have drifted away from biblical orthodoxy. InterVarsity Press for many years was a lifeline for Christians engaged in the intellectual battles of the universities and the secular culture. IVP still publishes books such as Phillip Johnson's *Darwin on Trial*, a work that broke through into secular circles to ignite fresh debates about evolution. But IVP also publishes "megashift" theology, as in *The Openness of God* and other works by Clark Pinnock, which maintains that God changes, that he condemns no one, and that salvation is possible apart from faith in Christ.

William B. Eerdmans for many years was one of the relatively few publishers to specialize in solid, scholarly research from the perspective of conservative Protestantism. Eerdmans still publishes on occasion important evangelical books such as David Wells' *No Place for Truth*, but it also puts out books from the perspective of contemporary liberal theology, Roman Catholicism (including hagiographic lives of saints), and even Judaism (including a book on anti-semitism that argues, in the words of

25

the catalog, that "the New Testament itself expresses a deep distrust of the tradition into which Jesus was born").

Both InterVarsity and Eerdmans are interested in postmodernist theology, with its assumptions that theology in our "post-foundationalist" age is "constructed" rather than revealed. Again, such books may deserve to be printed, but why by the few publishers available for conservative Christian scholarship?

What has gone wrong in the Christian publishing industry can perhaps best be illustrated in the career moves of Mr. Peretti, the million-selling author. Word lured Mr. Peretti away from Crossway, the company that launched his career, for a reported $4 million and a plan to turn Mr. Peretti into a crossover hit, helping him to break into the coveted secular market.

According to a veteran publishing insider who spoke on condition of anonymity, Word took the first manuscript Peretti delivered, *The Oath*, and hired a secular editor from the New York publishing establishment to make it more acceptable for the tastes of the non-Christian market. As might have been, *The Oath* has failed to win the big sales of Mr. Peretti's first novels. Apparently, it has not attracted the attention of Stephen King fans, for many of whom overt evil is what is titillating. Nor has it won much favor from Peretti fans, who find that it lacks what attracted them to his writing in the first place. Spokesmen for Nelson/Word did not return *World*'s calls seeking comment.

The irony is that, in all of the attempts by the Christian publishing industry to reach the secular world by emulating its values, it is failing to do so. Despite phenomenal sales and a dramatic growth of market share, Christianity is not exerting an increasing influence on the culture. It is the other way around. Some Christian publishers tend to think that being too explicit about issues of faith is the main barrier to crossover acceptance. They forget that the Christian writers who have won the greatest reputation in secular circles—such as T. S. Eliot, C. S. Lewis, and Flannery O'Conner—have been in your face about their faith, winning attention by the power and originality of their writing.

Judging by the buzz at past conventions, conversations with practically anyone at this year's CBA convention—authors, editors, marketers, booksellers—will uncover a host of frustrations, bitter experiences, and disillusionment. Most of the individuals committed to the industry still have a strong sense of Christian vocation and hope to publish books of genuine value. But if past conventions are a guide, insiders will swap tales of ruthless competition, ghostwriting in high places, and regrets about things they believe they had to do.

One insider even ruefully observes that in some ways Christian publishing is more [cutthroat] than its non-Christian equivalent, since federal and state laws provide remedies for such conflicts as contract violations and intellectual property disputes. Christians in the industry, to their credit, usually continue to follow the scriptural injunction not to sue fellow Christians. The apostle Paul's warning against lawsuits was not intended, of course, as a cloak for shady dealings. Rather, it was predicated on the fact that Christians should be above the concerns of mere worldliness. It also assumed the accountability of church discipline.

The revival of Christian publishing must be, above all, a spiritual revival, for which Christians should be praying. In the meantime, the church can still hold the publishers of its Bibles and its ideas accountable. The power of the marketplace can exert a positive as well as a negative influence. Christian retailers can become more selective about what they stock. Christian book buyers can be better stewards, spending their money not on spiritual junk food but on what is true to the Bible.

Christians, after all, are people of the Book. Since God reveals himself by means of a Book, some of those at the CBA convention next week will be praying not for the opportunity to surf the newest big wave, but for God to safeguard and review the acts of writing, publishing, and reading.[4]

Should you self-publish? Given the current direction of Christian publishing, it may be your only option. It should be something you seriously pray over. Ask the Lord to confirm the direction you should take with your specific project. Consider this article from *U.S. News & World Report.*

Former Milwaukee salesman Fred Gosman couldn't interest a publisher in his book on why parents should stop spoiling their kids. "You're no expert," he was told. But Gosman figured that being a parent was expertise enough. So, after being rejected by [twenty] or so publishers, he decided he would publish *Spoiled Rotten: Today's Children and How to Change Them* on his own.

Gosman, whose book has since sold tens of thousands of copies, is in good company. "Self-publishing is the fastest-growing segment of the publishing industry," says Jan Nathan of the Publishers Marketing Association [PMA] trade group. Self-publishing works best with how-to books and carefully targeted niche markets. Atlanta author Diane Pfeifer, for example, has successfully produced two specialty cookbooks, fewer than half of which have been sold in bookstores. Pfeifer netted $110,000 on *For Popcorn Lovers Only*, published in 1987. She rushed to print with *Gone with the Grits* in four months so it could debut last April at the World Grits Festival in St. George, SC. She is also peddling the book in airport and hotel gift shops and turnpike restaurant chains.

BOOK VALUE

Getting your name in print isn't cheap. "Putting out a book costs about $12,000," says Dan Poynter, self-published author of more than [sixty] books including *The Self-Publishing Manual* ($19.95, Para Publishing, 1997). But compared with the standard 10 to 15 percent royalty that publishers traditionally offer authors, self-publishers can pocket up to 30 percent. Of course, you'll eat up much of the royalty on production costs. "You're not going to make enough money on one book to leave another career," says the PMA's Nathan.

Self-publishers can be as involved as they choose in the nitty-gritty of book production. Once the manuscript is written, a modem can transmit it over phone lines to the typesetter. But hands-on authors can produce the entire opus in their home office with the right computer setup. Typesetting at home can save weeks of time and as much as $6,000. The job demands software that can lay out and fit text around artwork—"PageMaker," "Ventura Publisher" or "Quark XPress" will do and can cost $500 or less on sale—and a laser printer that will produce camera-ready copy that can be taken right to the printer.

Harried authors may find it worthwhile to farm out production to a pro. About Books in Buena Vista, Colorado, for instance, charges $12,000 to $40,000 for everything from editing to designing the cover and registering the copyright. Such consultants are different from vanity publishers. Book consultants work for a preset fee; profits are yours. Vanity publishers offer only a royalty after charging you to produce the book; complaints about quality and marketing are legion.

COOKING UP A SALES PLAN

Many self-published writers are surprised to learn that their biggest job begins after the book is printed. Marketing demands cunning, stamina, and luck. When cookbook writer Pfeifer couldn't interest Macy's book buyers in a book signing, she arranged one through the gourmet department instead. *Spoiled Rotten* author Gosman lived in his car and in cheap motels for weeks, pitching his book to newspapers, radio, and television. Gosman's grueling schedule paid off when the publicity led to an offer to publish the book from Villard Books, a subsidiary of Random House, and an advance in the high five figures. Craig Zirbel, who wrote *The Texas Connection: The Assassination of John F. Kennedy*, credits providence for his stints on the New York Times and other best-seller lists. "It's like I was sitting in the ballpark waiting for the game and someone threw me the ball and I hit a grand slam. It's pure dumb luck."[5]

Now, this book is a guide to *Christian* self-publishing, and that was a secular article. You and I both know it's not about luck—it's about hearing God and being obedient to what He tells us to do. When we obey, He blesses. But I am trying to make a point for self-publishing, because if the secular industry is saying self-publishing is the fastest growing segment, then the same will be true in Christian publishing. It is a fact that the trends in the secular book publishing market set the pace for the Christian book publishing market.

Now don't tuck tail and run. You don't have to spend $40,000 to get a quality book into print. As I mention in chapter 2, this tends to be a greed-driven industry, but that does not mean that all Christian subsidy publishers, book packagers, and consultants are dishonest. In fact, you'll see a list of my personal recommendations of fair and reputable professionals listed in appendix 1.

Dan Poynter's best-selling book, *The Self-Publishing Manual,* gives us eight good reasons to self-publish.

Self-publishing is not new. In fact, it has solid early American roots; it is almost a tradition. Well-known self-publishers include Mark Twain, Zane Grey, Upton Sinclair, Carl Sandburg, James Joyce, D. H. Lawrence, Ezra Pound, Edgar Rice Burroughs, Stephen Crane, Mary Baker Eddy, George Bernard Shaw, Edgar Allen Poe, Rudyard Kipling, Henry David Thoreau, Walt Whitman, Robert Ringer, Spencer Johnson, Richard Bolles, Richard Nixon and many, many more. These people were self-publishers, though today the vanity presses claim their books were "subsidy" published.

Years ago, some authors elected to go their own way after being turned down by regular publishers, but today most self-publishers make an educated decision to take control of their book—usually after reading this book.

Do self-publishers ever sell many books? Here are some numbers (at last count): *What Color is Your Parachute?*, 4.3 million; *Fifty Simple Things You Can Do to Save the Earth*, 3.5 million; *How to Keep Your Volkswagen Alive*, 2.2 million; *Leadership Secrets of Attila the Hun*, over half a million; and *Final Exit*, over half a million copies. These authors took control and made it big.

Self-publishing is not difficult. In fact, it may even be easier than dealing with a publisher. The job of the publishing manager is not to perform every task, but to see that every task gets done. The self-publisher deals directly with the printer and handles as many of the editing, proofing, promotion and distribution jobs as he or she can. What they can't do, they farm out. Therefore, self-publishing may take on many forms depending on the author's interests, assets and abilities. It allows you to concentrate on those areas you find most challenging. . . .

HERE ARE EIGHT GOOD REASONS TO SELF-PUBLISH:

1. To make more money. Why accept 6 [percent] to 10 [percent] in royalties when you can have 35 [percent]? You know your subject and you know the people in the field. Certainly you know better than some distant publisher who might buy your book. While the trade publisher may have some good contacts, he doesn't know the market as well as you, and he isn't going to expend as much promotional effort. Ask yourself this question: Will the trade publisher be able to sell four times as many books as I can?

2. Speed. Most publishers work on an 18-month production cycle. Can you wait that long to get into print? Will you miss your market? The 1½ years don't even begin until after the contract negotiations and contract signing. Publication could be three years away! Why waste valuable time shipping your manuscript around to see if there is a publisher out there who likes it? Richard Nixon self-published *Real Peace* in 1983 because he felt his message was urgent; he couldn't wait for a publisher's machinery to grind out the book. Typically, bookstores buy the first book on a popular subject. Later books may be better, but the buyer will pass on them since the store already has the subject "covered."

3. To keep control of your book. According to *Writer's Digest*, 60 [percent] of the big publishers do not give the author final approval on copy editing. Twenty-three percent never give the author the right to select the title, 20 [percent] do not consult the author on the jacket design and 36 [percent] rarely involve the author in the book's promotion. The big New York trade publishers may have

more promotional connections than you, but with a stable of books to push, your effort may get lost in the shuffle. The big publishers are good at getting books into bookstores but they fail miserably at approaching other outlets. Give the book to someone who has a personal interest in it—the author.

4. No one will read your manuscript. Many publishers receive more than 100 unsolicited manuscripts for consideration each day. They do not have time to unwrap, review, rewrap and ship all these submissions, so they return them unopened. Unless you are a movie star, noted politician or have a recognizable name, it is nearly impossible to attract a publisher. Many publishers work with their existing stable of authors and accept new authors only through agents.

5. Self-publishing is good business. There are more tax advantages for an author-publisher than there are for just authors.

6. Self-publishing will help you to think like a publisher. You will learn the industry and will have a better understanding of the big picture. A book is a product of one's self. An analogy may be drawn with giving birth. The author naturally feels that his book is terrific and that it would sell better if only the publisher would dump in more promotion money. He is very protective about his book (ever try to tell a mother her child is ugly?). The publisher answers that he is not anxious to dump more money into a book that isn't selling. So, if the author self-publishes, he gains a better understanding of the arguments on both sides. It is his money and his choice.

7. You will gain self-confidence and self-esteem. You will be proud to be the author of a book. Compare this to pleading with people to read your manuscript.

8. Finally—you may have no other choice. There are more manuscripts than can be read. Most publishers don't have time to even look at your manuscript.[6]

In *Is There a Book Inside You?* Dan Poynter and Mindy Bingham offer a simple quiz to help you determine which route is best for you to go. The following should help to solidify some realistic expectations.

Publishing Options

Consider the following statements to help decide which publishing option is best for you.

CONVENTIONAL PUBLISHER
If you feel:
1. It is important to me to be published by a major New York publisher because I value the type of recognition that would bring.
2. I have a personal connection with a publisher. I know an editor and can get my manuscript considered.
3. Publishers and their editors will change my manuscript for the better. I trust their judgment.
4. I will be happy to accept a 10 percent royalty.
5. Rejection does not bother me. I will keep sending out my manuscript until I find the right publisher.
Then start trying to find a conventional publisher.

VANITY PRESS
If you feel:
1. I want a few copies of my book for family and friends. It does not have to sell.
2. I am not concerned about price or about getting a return on my investment.
3. I do not want to produce my own book.
Then a vanity press might serve your purposes well.

BOOK PRODUCER OR PACKAGER
If you feel:
1. I want an attractive, professional-looking book.
2. I want someone else to handle the details, to take my manuscript and deliver the books to me to sell.
A book producer might be your answer.

AGENT
If you feel:
1. I do not have the time to find a publisher.
2. I would rather create than sell.
3. I am confident of my talent as a writer.
You should try to find an agent.

SELF-PUBLISHING
If you feel:
1. I am businesslike as well as creative.
2. I can afford to invest in a business.
3. I want to maintain complete control over my book.
4. If I wait much longer, someone else will beat me to the market.
5. I want a business of my own, and I am willing to put in the time and effort necessary.
6. I want to maximize the return on my efforts.
Self-publishing might be the route for you.[7]

At this point, you may have prayerfully determined that self-publishing is the most viable option for your project. But before we move into the how-tos, I'd like to tell you some of the real-life successes and disasters that I've encountered working in this industry.

Two

SELF-PUBLISHING SUCCESSES & DISASTERS

A S I SPEAK ABOUT self-publishing across the country at Christian writers' conferences, I am amazed at the awful stories I hear. At every stop, someone has a tale about being taken advantage of by greedy and deceptive publishing companies. When the Lord gives you a message and you are passionate about writing it so that it will bless others, you may be especially susceptible to the unscrupulous motives of some vanity or subsidy presses. Some of those companies have the word _Christian_ in their names, but they don't act in a Christian manner.

It is no wonder that the whole arena of self-publishing has had a tarnished reputation. It is a serious offense when so-called Christian companies say they will help people get their work published, but instead take advantage of a writer's vulnerability. If you are going to consider spending your hard-earned money to publish your book, then God expects you to be a good steward of those resources. You should do your homework and not just publish with the first company that comes along and flatters you into signing a contract. Hopefully this book will help you to discern what's right for you and your manuscript—and your integrity.

In *subsidy* publishing the author pays for publishing his own book, and exorbitant prices are often charged. This is especially true for runs of 1,000 copies. In comparison, the price per book for 5,000 copies looks pretty good to the unsuspecting Christian writer. One company I know suggested a charge of approximately $9.00 each for 1,000 copies of a 144-page book, but their rate for 5,000 copies dropped all the way to $3.50. This is a big difference. Does the new author really need 5,000 copies of his book? Usually not, unless the author is in ministry or is doing a lot of public speaking. That kind of deception happens frequently in this industry. I consider this to be manipulation and an example of the "diverse weights and measures" of which the Bible warns. Proverbs 11:1 says, "Dishonest scales *are* an abomination to the Lord, but a just weight *is* His delight."

A few years ago, before WinePress had any distribution and marketing capabilities, a pastor who had been considering our services decided to go to another company that promised to list his book in their catalog. The last time I saw him he hung his head sheepishly as he admitted to sending this "Christian" company $9,000 six months before. At that point he had not heard one word from them, but his check had been cashed.

Another retired pastor who was a longtime acquaintance decided that a different subsidy publisher could offer him more because they also promised his book would go into their catalog. Based on their assurance of great sales, he paid close to $20,000 for 5,000 copies of his book. He was a retired pastor! He was not doing any speaking or ministry that would get him in front of prospective buyers.

Given his situation, WinePress would have suggested he start with a run of 1,000 copies—to see if his book would sell well—and then consider reprinting later. We would have suggested that he do a *test run* to assess the market. This retired pastor still has a garage full of books and is desperately doing all he can to get media exposure in order to sell them. This is just another horror story of greed-driven manipulation.

While speaking at a Christian writers' workshop last year, I met Joyce. She told me the sad story of how she found a subsidy publisher from Georgia in the *Christian Writers' Market Guide*. They initially quoted her a reasonable price to publish her book, but in the end she paid $5,000 for 400 copies. The cover was ugly, the spine was crooked, it had no *ISBN* (International Standard Book Number) that all reputable publishers assign to every book, and quite frankly, it looked like it had been assembled by amateurs in a garage.

While at the American Christian Writers' Conference in Orlando, Florida, I met with another retired minister. He was so excited about the letter he had received from a publisher that told him what a wonderful manuscript he had. They assured him it needed to be published. With the letter they included a contract to publish 1,000 copies of his book for $14,000! Of course, they offered to market it. But after taking his money up front—more than double the actual cost of book production—I doubt they would have any incentive for making a significant marketing effort.

At Marlene Bagnull's Greater Philadelphia Christian Writers' Conference, I met a wonderful man from Ethiopia. He had been in the United States five years and was in full-time ministry. He told me how he had responded to a secular vanity press advertisement in a Christian publication. At the time that I spoke with him, he had spent $18,000 for 3,000 books. The cover was unprofessional at best, and any copies that he wanted to have or sell, he had to purchase from the company. That is highway robbery! When the book didn't sell during the first year, the vanity press destroyed the inventory after offering him a chance to buy back his books for another $6,000.

Very recently I spoke to a friend who ghostwrites for people in ministry who have a story to tell but don't have the time or expertise to write their own book. He shared with me that one pastor he was working with took his manuscript to a cooperative publishing group out of Tulsa, Oklahoma. He paid them $30,000 for 10,000 copies. Among other things, they changed the Scripture references from the King James Version to another version without his approval. He is suing them to get his money refunded, having pulled the job because he felt they were not acting in an ethical manner.

We continue to meet pastors and people in ministry who have had their books packaged by reputable companies but are paying $3,000 to $10,000 more than WinePress would charge. We hear countless stories of people paying too much money for an inferior product, resulting in a garage full of books. It is amazing to see how greed-driven this industry is, even when the companies *are* reputable and actually deliver what they promise.

Yet, there are also some real success stories, proving that you don't need to despair about ever getting your manuscript published.

I'll start with our own story. Back in 1988, my husband, Chuck, wrote a manuscript for Vietnam veterans dealing with post-traumatic stress disorder, telling in the book how the Lord healed him when he surrendered to Christ.

At the time, we were in full-time ministry running Point Man Ministries, an international organization. When Chuck tried to interest some publishers in the concept of his book, he continually received rejection letters. One agent in New York said the manuscript was not marketable, stating, "Veterans don't read." It would have been easy to quit at that point, but we knew that the message needed to be in print and that the book would be helpful for the ministry. I don't think we realized at the time how important a published book was going to be in terms of media exposure and credibility. We just knew we needed to offer this information as a resource. There were thousands of veterans who had expressed a strong need for this kind of help.

The first miracle we experienced was when we were contacted by a man who worked at a Christian royalty publishing house in the Midwest. He had a burden for veterans and offered to edit the work and get it "packaged" for us. He had the cover designed, the text typeset, obtained an ISBN, and printed 10,000 copies for $1 apiece. A Korean Christian businessman donated the $10,000 we needed to print the book, which was the second miracle!

When Chuck's book, *Nam Vet: Making Peace with Your Past*, came out he immediately became identified as an expert. He was called on to appear on local TV and radio stations for interviews, and the books quickly flew out the door. We were speaking at various churches almost every weekend. With a book table in the foyer, we gave people a way to buy copies to send to their veteran family members. Within two years we had sold all 10,000 books.

Toward the end of the second year, we were interviewed on an international television program, *The 700 Club*. While we were waiting in the greenroom we met a man named Rob Michaels, who represented the Christian music group Degarmo and Key. He had a tremendous burden to see Vietnam veterans set free and asked if he could present the book to some major publishers. Since all the money taken in from book sales had gone into the ministry, this was a third miracle.

Within just a few weeks Rob attended the National Religious Broadcasters (NRB) convention in Washington, DC. On the last day he just happened to bump into Larry Libby, the senior editor for Multnomah Press. He gave the editor the book, told him of its track record of selling 10,000 copies over the previous two years, and asked him to consider buying the rights.

Larry read the book on the plane trip home to Oregon and called Chuck as soon as he walked in the door. Little did Rob know that Larry's brother was a Vietnam veteran. He was so moved by the book he offered to buy the rights and offered a $5,000 advance. That was in 1990. They redesigned the cover, did a few touchups to the text, and printed 7,500 copies right away. Eight years later they have just completed their eighth printing, and the book has sold over 50,000 copies. Countless numbers of veterans have been saved along the way.

In August of 1995 I completed my first manuscript, *Consumed by Success: Reaching the Top and Finding God Wasn't*

There. I wrote it in obedience to a message that I felt the Lord had given me. He wanted me to expose the plan of the enemy, who keeps Christians so busy chasing the American Dream that they lose the most important thing in life: their first love, Jesus. It is definitely a controversial message and a hard word for the body of Christ. In the book I admit how I nearly destroyed my friendships, family, and faith by getting consumed with multilevel marketing. I didn't write it to make money and would give all the books away if I could afford to do so. To keep my motives right, I have designated all my royalties to two different ministries. I wrote it because I had a burning passion inside to see others set free from the unhealthy pursuit of success—just as I had been.

The first printing was 2,500 copies of the original ninety-six-page manuscript. Out of that I gave away about 700 copies. I did nearly 100 radio and TV interviews from November to April, including *Money Matters* with Larry Burkett, *Prime Time America* with Jim Warren, and many other national and regional Christian talk shows.

As I did those interviews, the Lord continued to give me new insights to share during the interviews. Since most of the shows encouraged telephone calls from the audience, I heard hundreds of stories of others who had been deceived and victimized by the "get-rich-quick" programs that are running rampant through our churches. I knew after only a few months that I had enough material for an updated edition.

Having done more speaking than writing, I had never really considered myself to be a writer. I knew that if I wanted the book to be a quality work as well as a convicting message for the body of Christ, I would need some help. So I got together with an editor who helped strengthen the weak parts of the book and enhance the rest with additional dialogue and real-life stories of others who had experienced the same things. The revised and expanded edition came out in May 1996 at 192 pages. With a new cover and a stronger message than ever, it is continuing to touch people where they live.

As we were going into our second printing, I whined to the Lord, "Why can't we just get a publisher to buy it? Just think what another self-publishing success story would do for WinePress!"

But the Lord made it very clear to my heart that selling the book to a major publisher could end up misleading many people into the unrealistic expectation that if they just published with WinePress they would automatically get picked up by a major publisher. He impressed upon my heart that I needed to be faithful to practice what I preached, be an example for others, and have a successful self-published book that stays self-published for the time being.

I repented for my whining and got on with the matters at hand. At this time we are close to going back to press for the fourth time within twenty-four months. *Today's Christian Woman* and *CharismaLife* have featured articles based on the book in recent issues, and *The Plain Truth* will be running an excerpt in the summer of 1998. *The Bookstore Journal* (a Christian bookstore trade publication) also ran a book review in a recent issue. As I continue to be faithful with the message He has given me, God is faithful to open the doors needed to get the message out.

The account of how the Living Bible was published is another amazing story. Back in the early sixties, Ken Taylor completed his new translation of the Bible. He shopped it around to different publishers and got nothing but rejections. He believed so strongly in the project that he printed up 2,000 copies on his own. It wasn't long before Billy Graham obtained a copy and held it up at a crusade. The rest is history! Tyndale House Publishers hit the map in the publishing industry as the result of this self-published book.

Joseph Girzone is another self-publishing victory in the Christian publishing world. His novel, *Joshua*, was rejected many times. He published it himself and sold 60,000 copies before selling the rights to a major publisher. Since that time he has written a number of successful sequels.

Dynamic minister T. D. Jakes self-published his first few books through a subsidy publisher. One of those books, *Woman, Thou Art Loosed*, hit the Christian bestseller list. Now Jakes is being actively pursued by many major publishers.

Maggie Kinney of Dallas, Texas, has been helping local authors self-publish for many years. In 1993 her pastor had an idea for a book of quotations about God and America and began putting the information together. She packaged the book for him, and they named it *America's God and Country*. Since that time they have sold more than 100,000 copies. They're not interested in selling it to a publisher—they're doing just fine without one!

Consider the phenomenal story of *The Christmas Box*.

> The saga of The Christmas Box has only begun. Utah advertising writer Richard Paul Evans originally printed [twenty] copies of his short parable about a parent's love for a child to share with family members. When people around his home began asking local bookstores for it (one bookseller received [ten] orders for it), Evans decided to find a publisher. After repeated rejections ("uncategorizable," "too long," "too short"), he published himself, starting with 3,000 paperback copies distributed mainly in the West. By the time Simon & Schuster bought hardcover rights in a frenzied auction last February, Evans had sold 700,000 copies.[1]

Other self-publishing successes include *The One-Minute Manager, What Color Is Your Parachute?* and *Managing from the Heart*, plus many secular blockbusters, like *The Celestine Prophecy, Mutant Message Down Under*, and *Surfing the Himalayas*.

I don't want to give a false hope that every self-published author should expect to get picked up by a royalty publisher. It has happened to some, but to most it does not. The article "Self-Publishing Successes" cited above, notes that larger publishers are always on the lookout for successful books. However, I would encourage you to look at the possibility of self-publishing as an end in itself. If you expect to self-publish with the intention of being picked up by a royalty house, your expectation is an unrealistic one and you are bound to be disappointed. The self-publishing experience should be a positive one for you, not a nightmare! To begin with, you need realistic expectations along with pure heart motives.

Three

WHAT'S YOUR HEART MOTIVE?

WHY DO YOU WRITE? Have you ever thought about your bottom-line motivations for becoming a published author? Scripture states, "The heart *is* deceitful above all *things*, and desperately wicked; who can know it?" (Jer. 17:9). We need to be willing to ask the Lord to purify our motives and to warn "if there is any wicked way" in us (Ps. 139:24). If we truly want the Lord to use our writing to minister to others, we must ensure that our writing flows from a clean and pure heart.

Why do you write? Is it for personal enjoyment? Is it to aid in and record your spiritual growth? (Journaling is a good example of this.) Is it to earn part- or full-time income (tentmaking)? Is it to teach or help others? Or is it for ministry purposes? Once you have established your reason for writing, ask the Lord to purify your motives.

No matter what we do in life, it is going to be motivated by one of two things: God or self. I know that sounds hard, but think about it. In everything we do, we are striving to please either ourselves or God. When our motives truly become selfless instead of selfish, and we begin to seek God's face and hear directly from Him on what we are to write and how we are to write it, we can be sure that the Lord will bring life to those who read our work.

Another area that must be checked is the root of our message. Are we telling our story to make a killing (greed)? To set the record straight (anger)? To right a wrong (unforgiveness, bitterness, or revenge)? To see our name in lights (pride)? Because something terrible may happen if we don't get this word out (fear)?

A woman once asked us to design and publish her book. It had already been mentioned in a denominational magazine as a "must read," and she was adamant that we help her get it into book form. It turned out that the book was an exposé of a denomination's financial mismanagement at their regional headquarters, which resulted in many pastors losing their retirement income after years of faithful service in the ministry. The more I listened to this woman, the more evident it became that her manuscript was written out of revenge and bitterness. She was the wife of one of those pastors and wanted to tell the truth so that the denomination would take responsibility for its sin. Even though she had her money in hand and wanted WinePress to publish her book, I knew that God would not honor that message if it was written from a root of bitterness. We chose not to co-labor in that particular project since it would have given God's work a "black eye" in our area of the Pacific Northwest. Even though we could have used the money at the time, I knew the Lord would bring other jobs to meet our obligations.

Sometimes I meet people in the Christian publishing world who turn their noses up at self-publishing with the attitude: "I wouldn't even consider spending my own money to print my books. I wouldn't lower myself to that." I see pride written all over their faces and am always saddened that people confessing to be Christians could be so puffed up and full of self.

The root of pride is visible when writers tell me they are convinced God gave them their manuscript word for word and it doesn't need any editing. Sometimes I want to ask, "If the God who dictated your book is the same God of the universe who created all things, then how

46

come He doesn't know how to spell?" We need to be willing to be teachable and to take honest criticism so that our work becomes the best that it can be for God. Joining a Christian writers' critique group may be the first step in crucifying the flesh, dealing a death blow to our pride, and being willing to be accountable to others who are going in the same direction with their writing.

In 1995, while I was teaching at Seattle Pacific University's writers' conference, I heard a creative song with a lot of truth. It was written by two attendees.

If I Were an Author
© 1995 by Margaret D. Smith and Janet Lee Carey
Used by permission

(To the tune of "If I Were a Rich Man")

If I were an author
Diga-diga-diga-diga-diga-deeze.
All day long I'd fax a little book,
Keep Oprah on hold,
Stacking up my royalties.

I wouldn't have to work hard
With my staff of twelve to handle all my
photographic crew.
All day long I'd think immortal thoughts,
Make up brilliant plots,
With characters too vivid to be true.

Bridge:
I'd call my publishers at home at midnight
Just to chat a little bit.
They'd have to sit and listen to all my dreams.
And when *New Yorker* came to beg forgiveness
For ignoring childhood genius in my poems,
I'd grant them an exclusive interview.
Ya-da-da-dee-da-da
Ya-da-da-dee-da-da

I wouldn't be rejected,
Neener-neener-neener-neener-neener-neener-neener-
noo.
Everyone would ask for my next book,
I'd keep them on the hook,
And tell them I had better things to do . . . like . . .
Going on vacation
To the south of France or maybe on a little yacht in
Spain.
Hey here comes the mailman with my book,
Here, let's take a look. . . .
Guess I'll have to send it out again.

Bridge:
Until they finally recognize my potential,
Talent dripping from my every pore,
I'll have to stop this song and write . . .
Some . . . more!

Ya-da-da-da-da-da
Ya-da-da-da-da-da-da-da-da-da-da-da-da-da-da

Hiya!

This song makes gentle fun of the vain imaginations of
seeing our name in lights! If our motivation is rooted in pride,
sooner or later we will be disappointed!

Is your motive to get published, no matter what it takes?
To see your name on a book, whatever the cost? To be an
author rather than "merely" a writer?

Sometimes, when participating on editorial panels at various Christian writers' conferences, I hear interesting suggestions offered by Christian publishing "experts." Someone
in the audience may ask what the represented publishing
houses are looking for in the way of publishable material.
Inevitably someone on the panel will suggest that the person
do his homework and see what is selling in the American
Booksellers Association (ABA) market, the secular counterpart to the Christian Booksellers Association. Once they de-

termine what is selling there, they should assume a similar trend is in the future for the Christian market and write toward that end. Only rarely do I hear editors on these panels encourage Christian writers to write from their passion.

Writing may or may not turn out to be a profit-making venture, but for Christians, writing is a ministry aimed at bringing life to those who read the message. If we are not anointed by the Holy Spirit to write on a subject, then it will all be the "wood, hay and stubble" that 1 Corinthians 3:12 speaks about. Yes, you might be able to sell the manuscript to a publisher, but unless it has come as a result of the passion burning within you to share the message God has given you, it will fall short of the glory of God. It will be just another book with no anointing, no power through the Holy Spirit to bring change to its readers.

These words may be offensive to some who make their living cranking out books for major Christian publishers, but as Leonard Goss shared at a writers' conference in Philadelphia:

> . . . in Christian publishing, our sense of business may be taking over our sense of critical [judgment]. Maybe you have heard the phrase *the publisher's smell.* The publisher's smell is what we feel comfortable publishing. I'm afraid that the publisher's smell may be changing—even in Christian publishing. Many in Christian publishing today are unconcerned about the right choice of what to publish. Rather, they are concerned only with sales and with bringing their wares to the market. This is the jackpot syndrome. When George Bernard Shaw once said of publishing that, "There is probably no other trade where there is so little relationship between profits and actual value or into which chance so largely enters" he had no clue what would become of Christian publishing in the 1990s, but Shaw certainly described Christian publishing in the 1990s. Now the idea is to package the books right so that they appeal only to the very general reader representing the blasé Christian mainstream. The idea is simply to publish more books that sell more and fewer books that have a limited

reading audience. The idea is to compete with the electronic media for the entertainment dollar, to bring all the glitz and all the visual appeal to books that one associates with the electronic media.

We need to learn to wait on God, hear His voice, and use the gift of writing in the way He instructs, not just plot what will sell or dream up a good idea or crank out a formula. We must learn to sit at Jesus' feet and let Him refine us, mold us, purify us, and make us a vessel of honor. Then—and only then—can He use us to be effective messengers with the words He gives us.

INDUSTRY TERMS

T HE VOCABULARY OF the publishing industry may seem like a foreign language when you're first starting out. Sometimes I throw around terms assuming everyone knows what I'm talking about. Thankfully, someone will always bring me back down to earth by asking, "What is a *subsidy* publisher?" I think it would be a good idea to clarify some of the terms we have mentioned in the first few chapters. These definitions are excerpted from Dan Poynter's book, *The Self-Publishing Manual*.

THE BIG PUBLISHING FIRMS are like department stores; they have something for everyone. They publish in many different fields and concentrate on books that anticipate audiences in the millions. . . . They put up the money, have the book produced, and use sales reps to get it into bookstores, but they will not promote the book. The author must do it. . . . They pay you an average of 15 [percent] on the wholesale price collected for your book. . . .

VANITY OR SUBSIDY PUBLISHERS [also called *custom* publishing and *contract* publishing] offer regular publishing services, but the author invests the money. . . . ($10,000 to $30,000). [Authors receive 40 percent of the retail price of the books sold.] . . . They don't make any promises regarding sales and usually the book sells fewer than 100 copies. The vanity publisher doesn't have to sell any books because the author has already paid him for his work. . . . Since binding is expensive, the subsidy publisher often binds a few hundred copies; the rest of the sheets remain unbound unless needed. The "advertising" promised in the contract normally turns out to be only a "tombstone" ad listing many titles in the *New York Times*. . . .

BOOK PACKAGERS are graphic arts shops that specialize in the production of books. They will edit the manuscript, design the book, set the type and lay out the pages. When the book is printed, it is delivered to you. Book packagers (or producers) do not invest in books, they do not promote books, and they do not store or ship books. They only put them together. . . .

LITERARY AGENTS match manuscripts with the right publisher and negotiate the contract; most new material comes to big publishers through them. The agent has to serve the publisher well, for if he or she submits an inappropriate or poor manuscript, the publisher will never offer another appointment. Therefore, agents like sure bets, too, and many are reluctant to even consider an unpublished writer. Their normal commission is 15 [percent]. . . .

According to *Literary Agent's Marketplace*, about:

40% of the book agents will not read manuscripts by unpublished authors, . . .

15% will not even answer query letters from them.

Of those agents who will read the manuscript of an unpublished author:

80% will charge for the service, but . . .

80% of the agents will not represent professional books;

93% will not touch reference works;

99% will not handle technical books;

98% will not represent regional books, satire, musicals and other specialized manuscripts;

    20% are willing to take on either novelettes or short
        stories;
    2% have a special interest in literature or quality
       fiction.

On the fringe, there are several "agents" who charge
a "reading fee," then pay students to read and critique the
manuscript. They make their money on the fees, not from
placing the manuscripts. . . .

SELF-PUBLISHING is where the author by-passes all the
middlemen, deals directly with the printer and then
handles the marketing and distribution. If you publish
yourself, you will make more money, get to press sooner
and keep control of your book. You will invest your time
as well as your money, but the reward is greater; you will
get it all.[1]

The statement "you will get it all" is true only if you choose
the right printer and know how to market and promote your
book without wasting your valuable time searching for the
answers to all your questions. The statement is true if you
don't spend too much money on the wrong advertising or
print more books than you could ever sell. There are many
books on the market about self-publishing and marketing
and distribution, but they are all geared to the secular market. If you try to market and distribute a Christian book
through secular channels, you will waste valuable time and
money.

Some additional industry definitions are:

COOPERATIVE PUBLISHING. A royalty publisher agrees to publish your book but requires you to collaborate in several specific ways.

    You, as the author, commit to purchasing half of the
5,000 print run at a 43 [percent] discount off the assessed
retail price of the book. The publisher retains the other

half of the print run in [a] warehouse for distribution. The author is paid a quarterly royalty on the sale of those books. The royalty percentage is determined before contract signing. The publisher uses all its resources to produce a high quality book. The author is required to do everything possible to help market and publicize the book, being available for radio and television interviews the publisher may choose to schedule.[2]

CHRISTIAN PUBLICIST. A person or company that specializes in booking media interviews for book authors on Christian radio and television. Publicists do not sell your book for you, they merely contact Christian radio and TV talk show hosts and producers and suggest your book as an upcoming topic to be addressed. They schedule as many interviews as possible for those authors who have an important message and the ability to communicate it. Some publicists work for a flat fee to promote an entire project, guaranteeing a minimum number of interviews for the fee; others charge a monthly fee plus expenses (shipping copies of your book to producers, long-distance calls, etc.) with a minimum of four to six months to complete the promotional campaign.

FULFILLMENT. The activity of receiving inbound telephone inquiries about your book. Typically a toll-free number is supplied, and operators are on duty twenty-four hours per day. Order processing is completed for people who order using a credit card, and product is packaged and shipped. If customers want to pay by check, the operator gives them the mailing address and total price, including shipping and handling. Product is warehoused by the fulfillment company, and either a per-piece/per-service item handling charge or a percentage of the retail price is deducted from the sales income monthly as a service charge.

These services are a great asset for authors who may have heavy media exposure or advertising and want to offer the convenience of a toll-free number to their potential customers. This is also helpful when a book is not readily available in the bookstore market but needs to be accessible to possible retail customers. The author can promote the book while someone else handles the details of answering phones, taking orders, processing charge cards, packing, shipping, and warehousing. However, remember that the fulfillment company doesn't sell your book—you have got to make that phone ring yourself!

CHRISTIAN BOOK DISTRIBUTORS. Companies that service the Christian bookstore market. Most Christian bookstore buyers are overworked and underpaid, and the last thing they want to do is buy books from every eager author who publishes his own book. For the most part, bookstore owners like to keep things simple: If a book isn't available through one of the major distributors, it isn't worth the hassle of carrying it in the store. The catch is that most of the Christian book distributors are pretty jaded about carrying self-published books, and rightly so. Many self-published books *look* self-published; and if a book looks bad, there is no way it can compete on the shelves of a Christian bookstore next to a book by someone like Max Lucado, whose publisher may spend $2,000 to $3,000 to create a cover that will "jump off the shelf" and into the customer's hand!

The bottom line is that it is not easy to have your book picked up by a distributor. While we at WinePress have contracts with all the major Christian book distributors, we will only send them titles that actually have the ability to compete nationally. The author must have a timely topic, the ability to communicate effectively via the media, and have a decent advertising/publicity budget. Most distributors expect a 55 to 60 percent discount so that they in turn can give a 40 to 45 percent discount to the Christian bookstores they serve. If a self-published author prints fewer than 5,000 copies, he cannot afford to give the discount required.

Five

BUDGETING YOUR PROJECT

BEFORE YOU START working on a budget for your project you need to thoughtfully ask yourself, "How many books should I print?" Typically, first-time authors overestimate rather than underestimate their sales. I would rather see someone print 1,000 or 2,500 copies and have to print more, than print 5,000 or 10,000 and end up with a garage full of books! Ask yourself the following questions:

1. Do you have an audience?
2. How are you going to reach them?
3. Are there any publications that zero in on that particular group?
4. Is your topic cutting edge or old news?
5. Are there any ministries or nonprofit organizations that promote a message similar to the one in your book?
6. Are you considered an expert in your field? (You don't have to have a Ph.D.)
7. Do you currently do any public speaking?
8. Have you done radio or TV interviews in the past?
9. Do you communicate effectively?

10. Do you have access to a mailing list of people who would need your book? (Targeted mailing lists are available for purchase, but you may already have a mailing list from your ministry activities, speaking engagements, etc.)
11. Do you have any other distribution channels through which your book might be sold?
12. Are you willing to spend additional money to promote and market your book?

By asking yourself these questions, you can get a feel for the number of books you should print. If the majority of your answers were no, you may want to consider printing just 1,000 copies and doing some test marketing with the book on your own. If nothing else, you will get your message out to a limited degree and will have fulfilled, without a huge financial outlay, the calling God had for you to get it into print. If you answered yes to at least five of the questions above, then you should seriously consider printing 2,500 copies. If you were able to give a positive answer to seven or more of the questions, then I would suggest printing from 5,000 to 10,000 copies, which would give you the best rate per copy. Remember, the higher the quantity, the lower the price per copy.

Here are a few sample budgets for small, midsize, and large print runs of books. I will use sample prices based on rates at WinePress Publishing. From my experience and comparisons they are the lowest in the industry—considering all the marketing helps and services that are included.

Small Run
1,000 copies—Suggested retail price $10 per copy

- 144-page book, 6" x 9"
- Copyedited and line proofed
- Formatted and typeset
- High-gloss, full-color custom cover
- Perfect bound (softcover)
- ISBN and Library of Congress number
- Press kits and some marketing helps
- Fulfillment services available
- Web page on the Internet

- Printed on 60 lb. white vellum paper
- Copyrighted in author's name
- Press releases to media within 200-mile radius

PRODUCT: $8,709

1. BOOKS: $7.69 each x 1,000 copies		$7,690
2. SHIPPING: (If all shipped to one address within domestic US; Hawaii and Alaska not included.)		$350
3. OVERRUNS: 100 x $6.69 (Potential for an additional 100 copies: 10%)[1]		$669

TOTAL: $7,690 + $350 + $669 ($7.92 each for 1,100 copies—assuming maximum overruns.)

MARKETING: $850

1. POSTCARDS: four-color x 1,000		$200
2. POSTAGE: $.20 x 1,000 postcards		$200
3. MAILING LIST: purchased		$150
4. MISCELLANEOUS: (Includes telephone calls, postage for giveaways, press releases, etc. Many radio stations expect authors to cover all long-distance costs.)		$300

TOTAL: $200 + $200 + $150 +$300

TOTAL PROJECT BUDGET: $8709 + $850   **$9,559**

At $10 per book you must sell 956 books at full retail in order to recoup your original expenses, which gives you money to reprint if necessary. Add to that about 25 giveaway books, and that leaves you with approximately 125 copies of your book remaining.

If you sold them all at the retail price, you would have $1,250 profit. Remember, if you don't make a lot of changes to the text pages or any changes to the cover art, your reprint cost per book should be somewhere in the neighborhood of $4.50 to $5.00 per book if you only print another 1,000. If you reprint 2,500, you could expect to pay about $2.50 to $2.75 per copy.

(Note: These figures are based on current rates. Paper prices and other costs will fluctuate in the future, so these prices should be considered approximate.)

Midsize Run
2,500 copies—Suggested retail price $10 per copy.
(Great for small to midsized ministries or those involved in speaking)

- 144-page book, 6" x 9"
- Copyedited and line proofed
- Formatted and typeset
- High-gloss, full-color custom cover
- Perfect bound (softcover)
- Printed on 60 lb. white vellum paper
- Copyrighted in author's name
- ISBN and Library of Congress number
- Press kits and some marketing helps
- Fulfillment services available
- Web page on the Internet
- Press releases to media within 200-mile radius

Regarding your suggested retail price, a nonprofit organization could offer its book for a suggested donation. Recently one of our authors, a full-time youth pastor, gave us a praise report of how a man gave him a $100 check for one book and another man followed with a $20 bill for a single copy of his $10 book.

Product: $10,080

1. Books: $3.57 each x 2,500 copies $8,925
(WinePress offers a special ministry discount of no charge for the four-color cover at this size print run. These prices reflect a $700 savings, assuming the author is in full-time ministry.)

2. SHIPPING: (If all shipped to one ad- $450
   dress within domestic US; Hawaii
   and Alaska not included.)
3. OVERRUNS: 250 x $2.82 (Potential for $705
   an additional 250 copies: 10%)

TOTAL: $8,925 + $450 + $705 ($3.66 each for 2,750 copies—assuming maximum over-runs.)

MARKETING: $2,900
1. POSTCARDS: four-color x 1,000 $200
2. POSTAGE: $.20 x 1,000 postcards $200
3. PUBLICIST: 4 months $1,600
4. MISCELLANEOUS $900

TOTAL: $200 + $200 + $1,600 + $900

TOTAL PROJECT BUDGET: $10,080 + $2,900   **$12,980**

At $10 per book you must sell 1,298 books at full re-tail price in order to recoup your original expenses. Add 250 giveaway books, and that leaves you with approxi-mately 1,200 copies of your book remaining. As we look at a scenario for a total print run you'll see that a profit is possible.

- 750 sold through the toll-free number $5,250
  at 30% discount
- 1,000 sold at retail through speaking $10,000
  engagements
- 750 sold at 50% discount for ministry $2,500
- 250 giveaways   N/A
- Total potential for the print run $17,750

POTENTIAL PROFIT
$17,750 income, less investment of $12,980   **$4,770**

Large Run 1
5,000 copies—Suggested retail price $10 per copy

- 144-page book, 6" x 9"
- Copyedited and line proofed
- Formatted and typeset
- High-gloss, full-color custom cover
- Perfect bound (softcover)
- Printed on 60 lb. white vellum paper
- Copyrighted in author's name
- ISBN and Library of Congress number
- Press kits and extensive marketing helps
- Fulfillment services available
- Web page on the Internet
- Press releases to media within 200-mile radius

PRODUCT: $13,430
1.	BOOKS: $2.36 each x 5,000 copies	$11,800
2.	SHIPPING: (If all shipped to one address within domestic US; Hawaii and Alaska not included.)	$700
3.	OVERRUNS: 500 x $1.86 (Potential for an additional 500 copies: 10%)	$930

TOTAL: $11,800 + $700 + $930 ($2.44 each for 5,500 copies—assuming maximum overruns.)

MARKETING: $12,400
1.	POSTCARDS: four-color x 5,000	$450
2.	POSTAGE: $.20 x 5,000 postcards	$1,000
3.	MAILING LIST: purchased	$375
4.	PUBLICITY AND ADVERTISING CAMPAIGN	$5,000
5.	MISCELLANEOUS	$1,600

TOTAL: $450 + $1,000 + $375 + $5,000 + $1,600

TOTAL PROJECT BUDGET: $13,430 + $8,425   **$21,855**

At $10 per book you must sell 2,185 books at full retail price in order to recoup your original expenses. Add to that 750 giveaway books and that leaves you with approximately 2,500 copies of your book remaining. Let's look at a possible scenario for the total print run.

• 1,000 sold through the toll-free number at 30% discount	$7,000
• 2,550 sold at 65% discount through distributors	$8,925
• 1,200 sold at retail through speaking engagements	$12,000
• 750 giveaways	N/A
• Total potential for the print run	$27,975

POTENTIAL PROFIT
$27,975 income, less investment of $21,855   **$6,120**

Large Run 2
10,000 copies—Suggested retail price $10 per copy

- 144-page book, 6" x 9"
- Copyedited and line proofed
- Formatted and typeset
- High-gloss, full-color custom cover
- Perfect bound (softcover)
- Printed on 60 lb. white vellum paper
- Copyrighted in author's name

- ISBN and Library of Congress number
- Press kits and extensive marketing helps
- Fulfillment services available
- Web page on the Internet
- Press releases to media within 200-mile radius

PRODUCT: $17,470

1. BOOKS: $1.52 each x 10,000 copies	$15,200
2. SHIPPING: (If all shipped to one address within domestic US; Hawaii and Alaska not included.)	$1,000
3. OVERRUNS: 1,000 x $1.27 (Potential for an additional 1,000 copies: 10%)	$1,270

TOTAL: $15,200 + $1,000 + $1,270 ($1.59 each for 11,000 copies—assuming maximum overruns.)

MARKETING: $21,700

1.	POSTCARDS: four-color x 5,000	$450
2.	POSTAGE: $.20 x 5,000 postcards	$1,000
3.	MAILING LIST: purchased	$375
4.	COOPERATIVE ADVERTISING: distributor mailings	$2,800
5.	PUBLICIST: 4 months	$1,600
6.	CBA AND NRB EXPOSURE	$2,000
7.	ADDITIONAL PROMO MATERIALS	$700
8.	MISCELLANEOUS: (Includes travel to NRB, CBA, and other events)	$6,000

TOTAL: $450 + $1,000 + $375 + $2,800 + $1,600 + $2,000 + $700 + $6,000

TOTAL PROJECT BUDGET: $17,470 + $14,925   **$32,395**

At $10 per book you must sell 3,917 books at full retail in order to recoup your original expenses. Add to that 1,000 giveaway books, and that leaves you with approximately 6,000 copies of your book remaining. Let's look at a possible scenario for the total print run.

• 1,500 sold through the toll-free number at 30% discount	$10,500
• 2,500 sold at 65% discount through distributors	$8,750
• 2,000 sold at 60% discount through nonprofit groups or ministries	$8,000
• 3,000 sold at retail through speaking engagements	$30,000
• 1,000 sold at special 25% discount	$7,500
• 1,000 giveaways	N/A
• Total potential for the print run	$64,750

POTENTIAL PROFIT
$64,750 income, less investment of $32,395   **$32,355**

A sample budget form has been included in appendix 2.

These examples should help you see how it is possible for you to get into print. One important point to understand is that you can't spend all your money printing books. You must be sure to budget enough money to promote and market the book. Plan to print fewer copies the first time and budget more for marketing and publicity. That way you'll actually *need* to go back to the presses again.

Now, before we take a look at what you'll need to be doing while the book is in the production phase, you're probably wondering, *Where in the world am I going to get that kind of money?*

RAISING FUNDS FOR YOUR BOOK PROJECT

O NE THING I KNOW for sure, our God owns the cattle on a thousand hills, and He's not broke! If He has called you to self-publish, He surely will provide the funds for you to do so.

I've seen Him do some pretty miraculous financing to ensure His children get His message into print. Maggie Kubo was thinking about taking out a loan to publish her children's book, *The Land of Broken Rainbows*. Right before she went that route, she received an unexpected inheritance that covered the exact cost of publishing her book! Jay Zinn put together a group of investors who believed in his end-times novel, *The Unveiling*. He promised them each a portion of the profits once the principal was paid back. So far, he's just about sold his original 8,000 copies and is ready to go back for a second printing!

Claire Vomhof had planned to publish his book of poetry for years but didn't have the funding. Recently a terminally ill man he knew offered to pay for the publishing so that Claire's dream could become a reality. The man died before he was able to give Claire the money, but his brother stepped up to the plate and donated the amount needed to get it into print. I could go on and on and on, but suffice it to say, He is able!

Recently I heard an interview with Harry Green of Advocate Media Group on this very topic. I pray that the ideas he shares are helpful to you.

Aside from any personal resources you may have, there are essentially three ways to generate capital to fund your project. They are sales, debt, and equity.

If you are fortunate enough to be able to get advanced orders for your product, you could fund your project with revenues produced by the sales. Because this is usually not possible, debt and equity funding represent the most used capital raising alternatives.

Debt—Borrowing money

Many people borrow money to finance their projects. Some people use their credit cards; others the equity line on their home; and some people borrow the money from friends, relatives, or a bank or credit union. I do not recommend this method of funding your project if you must rely on sales to repay your loan. I have seen many people experience great financial hardship when they counted on the sale of their product to bail themselves out of a financial jam.

If your motive for sharing your gift or producing your product is strictly to make money or to pay bills, you are headed for trouble. Everyone I have worked with who has elected to go this route has just dug themselves in deeper. Producing and marketing your product takes time, patience, and perseverance. Borrowing money can impose timetables on your project that are unrealistic or are unattainable. Moreover, if you borrow from friends or relatives you can really strain your relationships if things do not go as expected. If your family or friends want to help you, you're better off having them as investors and using an equity form of financing. This form of funding will define your relationship in a formal document and will clearly point out the financial risks and rewards inherent in their involvement in your project.

EQUITY FUNDING

If structured properly, an equity arrangement with investors who share your vision can be the best method of funding your project. Under this arrangement, you essentially sell a percentage of future revenue or ownership of your project in exchange for the money for production and marketing. This arrangement could be structured in the form of a limited partnership or a closely held corporation. Provisions for establishing partnerships and corporations vary by state. You should work with an attorney to establish the appropriate vehicle for your situation.

I believe that the limited partnership offers the most attractive source of funding for the entrepreneur who is an author, musical artist, or creative product producer. It provides unlimited flexibility for structuring percentage payback to investors while enabling the product creator or talent to maintain control or ownership. It also provides a formalized structure that appeals to investors.

The typical arrangement that appeals to investors involves paying them back their initial investment out of the first sales that are generated. Once they have regained their principal investment, their percentage is reduced to 10 or 15 percent of sales or profits while you retain the balance. This type of arrangement reduces the investors risk and enables them to participate in the long-term success of the project. Astute investors are always looking to reduce their downside risk and increase their upside potential. When you structure your deal, don't be greedy!

Try to get investors [who] can help you with more than money. People who believe in you that are constantly selling you are a great asset. People who put their "money where their mouth is" are by far the ultimate asset.

The limited partnership can also offer tax advantages to some investors. Your investors should seek the counsel of a good CPA or tax planner before you finalize the structure of your partnership. In this area, good advice is important. Don't try to save money by doing it yourself without the counsel of qualified professionals.

In addition to limited partnerships, there are a variety of corporate structures that can be considered as funding vehicles. I prefer partnerships in that they offer attractive methods for distributing revenues without selling the company or declaring dividends that could involve double taxation. The motion picture industry has been using partnerships for years to finance movies.

I cannot over emphasize the importance of seeking qualified counsel in structuring a financial relationship. Most states enable you to raise up to $1 million without registering your fundraising instrument with the Securities and Exchange Commission. Situations that involve fewer than [fifteen] investors are also usually exempt from such registrations.

Creating the right fundraising vehicle is not as complicated as it may seem and is one of the most important steps you can take in ensuring the success of your project. Some attorneys and accountants may work with you on a percentage basis and provide services you need for a "piece of the action." Do not be afraid to ask . . . but don't expect it. I have learned the hard way that you get what you pay for.

Once you have established your financial arrangement and secured capital from your investors, it is important that you continue to communicate with your investors on a regular basis. Keep them apprised of your progress. Call them regularly or send them a newsletter. Share the good news and the bad news. Don't make them call you.

More importantly, when you achieve success . . . if you achieve success . . . don't forget who brought you to the dance.

Thanks to Harry Green at Advocate Media Group—not only for the insight but also for the following documentation for limited liability partnerships. While I have not inserted the full-sized document into this book, the following is a good example of the legal wording used and the overall format for the paperwork. After this we'll take a look at some things you can do during the publishing process.

LIMITED LIABILITY
PARTNERSHIP AGREEMENT OF
_____ PROMOTIONAL PARTNERS, LLP

THIS LIMITED LIABILITY PARTNERSHIP AGREEMENT (the "Agreement") is made as of February _____, 1998, by and among _____

_____and
_____, (sometimes collectively referred to as the "Partners" or individually as "Partner"; the Managing Partner and the other Partners are sometimes referred to collectively as the "Partners").THE SECURITIES OFFERED HEREBY HAVE NOT BEEN REGISTERED UNDER THE SECURITIES ACT OF 1933, AS AMENDED (THE "FEDERAL ACT"), THE GEORGIA SECURITIES ACT OF 1973, AS AMENDED (THE "GEORGIA ACT"), OR THE SECURITIES LAWS OF ANY STATE, AND ARE BEING OFFERED AND SOLD IN RELIANCE ON EXEMPTIONS FROM THE REGISTRATION REQUIREMENTS OF THE FEDERAL ACT AND VARIOUS APPLICABLE STATE LAWS. IN ADDITION, THE TRANSFER OF THE SECURITIES IS SUBJECT TO THE RESTRICTIONS ON TRANSFER AND OTHER TERMS AND CONDITIONS SET FORTH IN THE LIMITED PARTNERSHIP AGREEMENT. THESE SECURITIES MAY NOT BE OFFERED FOR SALE, PLEDGED, HYPOTHECATED, SOLD, ASSIGNED, OR TRANSFERRED EXCEPT IN COMPLIANCE WITH THE TERMS AND CONDITIONS OF THE LIMITED PARTNERSHIP AGREEMENT. FURTHER, THESE SECURITIES MAY NOT BE OFFERED FOR SALE, PLEDGED, HYPOTHECATED, SOLD, ASSIGNED, OR TRANSFERRED UNLESS SUCH TRANSFER IS UNDER CIRCUMSTANCES WHICH, IN THE OPINION OF LEGAL COUNSEL ARE ACCEPTABLE TO THE PARTNERSHIP DO NOT REQUIRE THAT THE SECURITIES BE REGISTERED UNDER THE FEDERAL ACT OR ANY APPLICABLE STATE SECURITIES LAWS, OR SUCH TRANSFER IS PURSUANT TO AN EFFECTIVE REGISTRATION STATEMENT UNDER THE FEDERAL ACT OF ANY APPLICABLE STATE SECURITIES LAWS.

WHEREAS, the Partners desire to form a limited partnership pursuant to O.C.G.A. sec.14-8-62 and the Revised Uniform Limited Partnership Act of the State of Georgia; and

WHEREAS, the Partners desire to set forth their respective rights, duties, and responsibilities with respect to such limited partnership.

NOW, THEREFORE, for and in consideration of the mutual promises, obligations, and agreements contained in this Agreement, and other good and valuable considerations, the receipt and sufficiency of which are hereby acknowledged by each of the Partners, the Partners, intending to be and being legally bound, do hereby agree as follows:

1. Name of Partnership.
The name of the Partnership shall be _____
_____ Promotional Partners , LLP (the "Partnership").

71

2. Principal Office/Registered Agent.
The initial principal place of business and registered office of the Partnership shall be _____
_____.

The Partnership shall have such additional offices and may change its principal or registered office as the Managing Partner may designate. The initial registered agent of the Partnership is_____
_____.
Such registered agent may be changed from time to time by designation of the Managing Partner.

3. Names and Addresses of the Partners.

_____   _____
Managing Partner

_____   _____

_____   _____

_____   _____

4. Term.
The term of the Partnership shall commence upon the filing of a Certificate of Limited Liability Partnership with the Secretary of State of Georgia, and an election as provided in O.C.G.A sec. 14-8-62 and shall continue until the first to occur of the following: (a) December 31, 2002; (b) the election of the Partners to terminate the Partnership; (c) the sale by the Partnership of all of its assets, and the collection of all amounts derived from such sale, including all amounts payable to the Partnership under any promissory notes or other evidences of indebtedness derived by the Partnership from such sale; or

5. Purpose.
The purpose of the Partnership shall be (a) to promote artists and to sell their product(s) through television, radio and print media, and (b) to do any other lawful act permitted of the Partnership under governing law.

6. Capital; Percentage Interests.
(a) *Initial Capital.*

The initial capital contribution and percentage interest ("Percentage Interest") of each of the Partners is as follows:

Partners:	Capital Contribution:	Percentage Interest:
_____	$_____	_____%
_____	$_____	_____%
_____	$_____	_____%
_____	$_____	_____%
_____	$_____	_____%

72

(b) *Additional Capital.*

The Partners shall determine whether the Partnership requires additional capital in order to carry on its business. If the Partners unanimously determine such additional capital is required, such additional capital shall be contributed by the Partners pro rata and in proportion to their respective Percentage Interests in the Partnership.

(c) *Limited Liability.*

The Partners shall have no obligation to contribute or loan any capital whatsoever except as expressly provided in Subsection 6(b) above.

(d) *No Third Party Beneficiaries.*

The obligation of the Partners to contribute capital is solely for the benefit of the other Partners and the Partnership, and no third party shall have the right to enforce such obligations.

(e) *Capital Accounts.*

Separate capital accounts shall be maintained for each partner. Such capital accounts shall be maintained in accordance with applicable Internal Revenue Service Regulations.

7. Allocations of Profits and Losses and Distributions of Cash.

All allocations of profits and losses and all distributions shall be made to the Partners in accordance with their percentage interests. The Managing Partner shall determine when and if the Partnership has cash available for distribution to the Partners. The Managing Partner shall have the right to maintain reasonable reserves of cash for the partnership.

8. Management.

(a) Subject to the limitations hereinafter set forth, the Managing Partner shall have, and is hereby granted, the power, authority, and discretion to take such action for and on behalf of the Partnership, and in its name, as the Managing Partner shall deem necessary and appropriate, to carry out the purposes for which the Partnership was organized, it being expressly understood that except as hereinafter provided, the actions of the Managing Partner shall in all events bind the Partnership.

(b) The Managing Partner shall not have the authority to undertake the following actions unless such Partner has first obtained the consent of all the Partners:

(i) The creation of any mortgage, charge, or encumbrance on an asset of the Partnership other than any mortgage, lien, or encumbrance incurred in the ordinary course of business;

(ii) The sale of all or substantially all of the assets of the Partnership;

(iii) The acquisition, financing, refinancing, lease, or sale of any real property;

(iv) The execution of any contract or loan agreement pursuant to which the Partnership will make an aggregate investment exceeding $_____;

(v) The admission of any new partners in the Partnership; and

(vi) The undertaking, generally, to do any act which is in contravention of this Agreement or which would make it impossible to carry on the ordinary business of the Partnership.

(c) Any person dealing with the Partnership or the Managing Partner may rely upon a certificate signed by the Managing Partner, as to:

(i)   the identity of the Managing Partner or the other Partners;

(ii) the existence or nonexistence of any fact or facts which constitute conditions precedent to acts by the Managing Partner or which in any other manner are germane to the affairs of the Partnership; or

(iii) the persons who are authorized to execute and deliver any instrument or document of the Partnership.

(d) Unless unanimously agreed by the Partners, no partner shall be entitled to receive any salary, fee, draw, or other compensation for services rendered on behalf of the Partnership in his, her or its capacity as a Partner.

(e) Except as otherwise provided in this Agreement, the other Partners shall not take part in the management of the Partnership business or transact any business of the Partnership and shall have no power to sign for or to bind the Partnership.

9. Liability of the Managing Partner.

The Managing Partner, and his or its designees, shall have no liability to any other Partner by virtue of any action taken by such Managing Partner in good faith and shall have liability only for acts of bad faith, gross negligence, or willful misconduct. The Partnership hereby covenants and agrees to indemnify and hold harmless the Managing Partner and its designee from any and all liability incurred by him or it in connection with the carrying out of its duties hereunder; provided that such Managing Partner or its designee, as the case may be, shall not have acted in bad faith, have been grossly negligent, or have committed an act of willful misconduct; and provided further that any indemnity hereunder shall be provided out of and only to the extent of Partnership assets (excluding the obligation of the Partners to contribute additional capital) and undistributed income therefrom and the Partners shall not have any personal liability on account thereof.

10. Liability of the Other Partners.

Subject to any requirements hereunder to provide additional capital, the liability to the Partnership of the other Partners shall be limited to their interest in the assets of the Partnership and any undistributed income therefrom.

11. Transferability of Interests.

No Partner shall transfer, assign, pledge, or otherwise dispose of or encumber all or any portion of their interest in the Partnership without the prior written consent of all the Partners. Any permitted transferee of a Partnership interest must accept and agree in writing to be bound by all the terms and provisions of this Agreement and all amendments thereof.

12. Admission of Partners.
No additional partners shall be admitted to the Partnership without the consent of the Partners.

13. Banking.
All funds of the Partnership are to be deposited in a Partnership bank account in such financial institution as may be designated by the Managing Partner.

14. Location of and Access to Books of Account and Other Information.
The Partnership's books of account shall be kept at such locations as may be designated by the Managing Partner, and each Partner shall have access thereto at all reasonable times during business hours, and shall have the right to make copies thereof at such Partner's expense. Upon the request of a Partner, the Managing Partner shall provide or make available at the registered office of the Partnership during ordinary business hours:
(i)   a current list of the full name and address of each Partner;
(ii) a copy of the Certificate of Limited Liability Partnership and all amendments thereto;
(iii) copies of the Partnership's federal, state, and local income tax returns and reports, if any, for the four most recent years;
(iv) copies of this Agreement and all amendments hereto; and
(v)   other information regarding the financial condition and affairs of the Partnership as shall be reasonably requested by such Partner.

15. Tax Matters Partner.
The Partners hereby designate the Managing Partner as the "tax matters partner" in accordance with the applicable provisions of the Internal Revenue Code.

16. Competing Activities.
Nothing in this Agreement shall be deemed to restrict in any way the freedom of any Partner to conduct any business or activity whatsoever without any accountability to the Partnership or the Partners even if such business or activity competes with the business of the Partnership.

17. Liquidation.
Upon the occurrence of any of the terminating events set forth in Section 4 hereof, the Managing Partner shall convert the Partnership's assets into cash, and all such cash shall be applied and distributed in the following manner and in the following order of priority:
(a)   to the payment of the debts and liabilities of the Partnership and to the expenses of liquidation in the order of priority as provided by law; then
(b)   to the establishment of, or addition to, any reserves deemed necessary by the Managing Partner, for any contingent or unforeseen liabilities or obligations of the Partnership; provided, however, that any such reserves established hereunder shall be held in escrow for the purpose of paying any such contingent or unforeseen liabilities or obligations and, at the expiration of such period as the Managing

Partner deems advisable, of distributing the balance of such reserves in the manner provided hereinafter in this Section; then

(c) to the repayment of any liabilities or debts, other than Capital Accounts, of the Partnership to any of the Partners; and then

(d) to the Partners in accordance with their Percentage Interests. A reasonable time shall be allowed for the orderly liquidation of the Partnership's assets above in order to minimize the losses normally attendant upon such a liquidation. The Partnership shall be terminated and dissolved when all of its assets have been converted into cash, all promissory notes or other evidences of indebtedness derived by the Partnership from such conversion of its assets or otherwise have been collected or otherwise converted into cash, and all such cash has been applied and distributed in accordance with the provisions of this Section. The establishment of any reserves in accordance herewith shall not have the effect of extending the term of the Partnership, but any such reserves shall be distributed in the manner herein provided upon expiration of the period of such reserve.

18. Waiver of Right of Partition.

Each of the Partners does hereby agree to and does hereby waive any right it might have to cause any of the assets of the Partnership to be partitioned among the Partners or to file any complaint or to institute any proceeding at law or in equity to cause such partition.

19. Power of Attorney.

(a) Grant of Power. Each Partner does hereby irrevocably constitute and appoint the Managing Partner as his or her true and lawful attorney-in-fact, in their name, place, and stead, to make, execute, consent to, swear to, acknowledge, record, and file, in conformance with the terms and provisions of this Agreement, any certificate or amendment thereto or other instrument which may be required or appropriate to be filed by the Partnership or the Partners under the laws of the State of Georgia or under the applicable laws of any other jurisdiction, to the extent the Managing Partner deems such filing to be necessary or desirable to reflect the existence of the Partnership, the identities of the Partners, the dissolution and termination of the Partnership, or otherwise. Any third party may rely absolutely and without further inquiry on the power of attorney herein granted.

(b) Irrevocability of Power. The power of attorney herein granted to the Managing Partner is coupled with an interest, is irrevocable, by death or otherwise, and shall survive any assignment of a Partner's interest in the Partnership.

76

20. Investment Intent.

(a) Each Partner hereby represents, warrants, and acknowledges that:

(i) He is acquiring his interest in the Partnership solely for his own account for investment purposes and not with a view or interest of participating, directly or indirectly, in the resale or distribution of all or any part thereof;

  (ii) His interest in the Partnership is to be issued and sold to him without registration and in reliance upon certain exemptions under the Federal Act, the Georgia Act, and other applicable state securities law;

  (iii) He has received copies of the Partnership Agreement and he has had an opportunity to review it or have it reviewed by his representative;

  (iv) His investment in the Partnership has a high degree of risk and he has the net worth to sustain such risk; and

  (v) He will make no transfer or assignment of his interest in the Partnership except in compliance with the Federal Act, the Georgia Act, and any other applicable securities laws.

 (b) The Partners acknowledge and agree that a legend reflecting the restrictions imposed upon the transfer of their limited partnership interests under this Agreement, the Federal Act, the Georgia Act, and under any applicable state securities laws has been placed on the first page of this Agreement.

21. Miscellaneous.

 (a) Notices: Any notice, election, or other communication provided for or required by this Agreement shall be in writing and shall be deemed to have been received when delivered by hand or on the third calendar day following its deposit in the United States Mail, certified or registered, return receipt requested, postage prepaid, properly addressed to the person to whom such notice is intended to be given at such address as such person may have previously furnished in writing to the Partnership or at such person's last known address.

 (b) Modifications: No change or modification of this Agreement shall be valid or binding upon the Partners, nor shall any waiver of any term or condition in the future, unless such change or modification or waiver shall be in writing and signed by all of the Partners.

 (c) Binding Effect: This Agreement shall insure to the benefit of, and shall be binding upon, the Partners, their legal representatives, transferees, heirs, successors, and assigns.

 (d) Construction: This Agreement shall be interpreted and construed in accordance with the laws of the State of Georgia. The titles of the Sections herein have been inserted as a matter of convenience of reference only and shall not control or affect the meaning or construction of any of the terms and provisions hereof.

 (e) Pronouns: All pronouns and any variations thereof shall be deemed to refer to the masculine, feminine, neuter, singular, or plural, as the identity of the person or entity may require.

 (f) Entire Agreement: This instrument contains all of the understandings and agreements of whatever kind and nature existing between the parties hereto with respect to this Agreement and the rights, interests, understandings, agreements and obligations of the respective parties pertaining to the continuing operations of the Partnership.

 (g) Severability: Each provision of this Agreement shall be considered separable and if for any reason any provision or provisions herein are determined to be invalid, unenforceable or illegal under any existing or future law, such invalidity, unenforceability, or illegality shall not impair the operation of or affect those portions of this Agreement which are valid, enforceable, and legal.

IN WITNESS WHEREOF, this Limited Liability Partnership Agreement has been executed as of the date set forth above.

MANAGING PARTNER: _____(SEAL)

OTHER PARTNERS: _____(SEAL)

_____

_____

_____

_____

_____

END OF DOCUMENT

Seven

PREPUBLICATION PROMOTION

I T IS IMPORTANT to think about promotion during the production phase rather than waiting until the cartons of books are unloaded at your doorstep. I have outlined the important steps for you in order. Some suggested resources to help you with the following steps are listed in the back of this book.

GET THE WORD OUT

While you are writing your book you should be getting the word out. Tell everyone you know what you are writing about. Get people interceding for you and your project. If you know people at your local Christian bookstore, let them know what you are working on and when you plan to have your book completed.

INPUT

Be willing during the writing and editing process to get opinions, criticisms, testimonials, reviews, and comments. You want your message to be clear and your book to be the best possible. Be open to constructive criticism. Do not be close-minded or adamant that your message is exactly how God wants it written. Numerous rewrites are often necessary to ensure that your message is crystal clear. Go to people you *trust* (don't throw your pearls before swine!) and ask for their input. Once the manuscript seems close to completion, start collecting written reviews and testimonials from the people who read it. Be sure that you receive permission if you plan to use their comments in your sales material.

BOOK PRODUCTION

Now it is time to begin the production process. Submit your manuscript to a few reputable book packagers or consultants for a quote. After researching your options and getting at least three bids, start the process with the company that offers you a high quality product and the services you need for a fair price.

If you want to do it all yourself, you will need to begin the cover design first so that you have something to use when you create the sales literature. Then you will need to typeset the manuscript text into a *camera-ready* format that includes *crop marks*. (Be sure your software is capable of outputting postscript format with crop marks. A call to your local service vendor will let you know exactly what software will work.) During this time you will need to secure the following items to complete your package: an ISBN, Library of Congress number, bar code, and copyright. You will also need to begin getting bids from various printers or book manufacturers.

If all that seems a bit overwhelming to you, my best advice is to let someone help you. We did so with our first book. Again, it doesn't have to cost you an arm and a leg to "farm out" the production *if* you know what you're doing and what to watch for.

PRICE

It's a good idea to set a competitive retail price. Research similar products offered in the local Christian bookstores. One complaint bookstores have regarding self-published books is that they are typically overpriced. This is understandable when you realize how much some people have had to pay to get the job done! At WinePress we like to suggest that people use the following guideline:

Page Count	Suggested Retail Price
96–112 pages	$8.99
128–160 pages	$9.99
176–224 pages	$10.99
240–288 pages	$12.99
304–340 pages	$13.99
356–384 pages	$14.99
400–448 pages	$16.99

Because it is used for ministry, we set the price for *Nam Vet* at "any donation of $9 or more." It was amazing how many people gave us $10, $20, $50, and even $100 for one book. For those who are in the ministry full time, this is a great way to set the price of your book.

If you're going to be doing a lot of back-of-the-room sales after speaking engagements, you might set your price to one round figure that would include any applicable sales tax— such as, $10, $15, $20. This facilitates making change. In the seminar arena you can usually charge a little more for your book, and it will still sell because it is not competing with a hundred other books in a bookstore.

If you are going to sell your book mainly through a toll-free 800 or 888 number, or by mail order, you'll want to consider keeping the price lower. That way the total price, including your shipping and handling charge, won't scare off your customer.

PREPUBLICATION ORDER FORM

With your cover design completed, write some copy for a sales flier. Include prepublication ordering information, which offers people an incentive to purchase a copy before the book is published. Some authors offer a 20 to 25 percent discount and free shipping if people pay in advance to order the book.

Create a layout for the flier that includes the intended page count of the book, its retail price, ISBN, cover artwork, and an overview with reviews and comments. Also include the prepublication discount information and cutoff date, along with your other ordering information.

Pastor Ray Hampton started his project at WinePress with a 50 percent down payment on book production costs, and then, using a prepublication order form, raised the balance through prepublication sales. He was pleasantly surprised to discover how quickly he was able to cover the remaining cost of his project.

Press Releases to Local Media

Media exposure is a great way to get free advertising for your book. When creating your press release, there are a few things you need to consider. First, you must focus on how your book will benefit the reader. Work hard at capsulizing the content into 100 words or less, emphasizing the importance of your book's thesis. In your one-page press release, include reviews and positive comments about the book. (If WinePress is publishing your book, you will not need to do this, because our publicity department handles this for you.)

Once you have your press releases in hand, your next step is to search out suitable media contacts in your region and be persistent in following up. Concentrate on those who would naturally take an interest in your topic. Also, if you have a local Christian television station, you should contact them. They are usually very open to having local authors on their live show each week. Research and identify all the local Christian radio stations. One resource for this is the National Religious Broadcasters (NRB) annual directory. Find out if there is a local talk show or even a public service segment that would be open to an interview with a local author.

Page Proofs to Reviewers

If you are printing 5,000 or more copies, have committed to a publicity media campaign, and have an advertising budget/plan to make your book available in the Christian book-store market, then it is a good idea to send a copy of your *page proofs* (the typeset version of your manuscript) and a sample cover to the appropriate book reviewers. *Appropriate* means that if you are writing a book on moms leaving the workplace to stay home and raise their children, you wouldn't send your proofs to the book review editor for *Discipleship Journal*; you would send them to *Today's Christian Woman* or *Virtue* or *Christian Parenting Today*.

Remember, it's not easy to obtain a review. Don't get your hopes up that this is where all your sales are going to come from. I am very cautious in encouraging first-time authors toward this end, because the market is very competitive.

Some book reviewers are very picky about how they receive page proofs. They want them long before the book is released. Some even want them trimmed and bound. Again, unless you are printing 5,000 to 10,000 copies and will be doing a trade-market blitz with your book through the major Christian book distributors, I wouldn't spend a lot of time trying to get reviews in national Christian publications. You may, however, want to approach your local Christian newspaper to see if they would be interested in conducting an interview with you, using an excerpt from the book, or writing their own book review. Also, the religion editor for your local secular newspaper will often do book reviews.

Distribution Schedule

This step can be a Catch-22. If you are self-published, most Christian book distributors will not even look at your book. Spring Arbor Distributors are very direct with self-published authors. They tell you that it will take six months before they will even look at the finished product, and even then you should not count on them to pick it up.

I learned a lot in the process of distributing *Consumed by Success*. When you're self-published it seems like you have three strikes against you. Unfortunately, those out there who have created shoddy, unprofessional products have made it hard on the rest of us. Because WinePress has a commitment to the publicity and promotion of appropriate (truly market-able) titles, we have finally gained access to the major distribu-tors and have set up contracts with them for the titles we recommend. Again, this is not an automatic service for our authors, only one that is available when appropriate. Landing a Christian book distributor on your own is not altogether im-possible, but very close to it.

DIRECT MAIL CAMPAIGN

If you believe that the Lord wants you to promote and market your book by purchasing a mailing list of prospec-tive buyers, you don't want to wait too long to get started. My favorite direct mail campaign has been to use postcards. Since the cover artwork should now be completed, it can be used on the four-color glossy side of the postcard. The other side should have a short description of the book and a rea-son why people should buy it, along with simple ordering information: a toll-free number or an address, retail price, and shipping and handling charges.

The preference for using postcards is backed up by the statistics. A *Better Homes and Gardens* survey once found that an average of seventeen people read every postcard that is sent through the mail. That means sixteen people read your postcard before it actually gets to where it's going. That's awesome exposure!

When we started marketing Chuck's book, *Nam Vet: Making Peace with Your Past*, we created some postcards and mailed them to everyone on our Point Man mailing list. We received orders from all across the nation and found out lots of Vietnam veterans work in the US Postal Service. For a twenty-cent stamp and an eight-cent postcard—we printed 5,000—that was the best advertising we ever did.

FULFILLMENT SERVICES

While your book is in production, you'll want to be sure you are prepared to fill orders. Some of you may already have a merchant's account with Visa or Mastercard, an 800 or 888 number, and someone to answer your phones twenty-four hours a day. But most of you probably don't. If you want to be able to promote your book and not worry about the details of taking and filling orders, then you need a fulfillment service. Finalize this service ahead of time so you'll have the toll-free number to print in the back of your book and on all the promotional materials you are developing. Again, if you're publishing with WinePress, this is part of the service package.

BOOK SIGNINGS

Once you have a release date for your book, start organizing book signings with local Christian bookstores, your church, or other affiliated organizations. Sometimes Christian bookstores will have a Local Authors' Day, where they invite all the local authors in for a two- to-four-hour period to autograph copies of their books. The store promotes the event in the community so people can come in to meet the authors and buy autographed books. If your local Christian bookstore hasn't done this, suggest it to them.

Some of our authors have set up publication parties, where they send out invitations to everyone they know and announce the new publication. They make it a festive event. You may even have friends who would want to have a signing party in their home and invite all their friends over to meet you and hear about your book. Through scheduling events such as these, you'll find many opportunities to share the message the Lord has given you.

If your release date is October 1 and you expect to have your books in hand a week or two before that, build in some extra time as a buffer. We had one author who was expecting to receive his books on December 1 (a Friday). He set up an autographing party and invited a lot of people for the following Monday. Wouldn't you know it, the truck carrying his books broke down in Phoenix, and they couldn't get the part needed until Monday morning. Fortunately we had sent him five copies of the book on Thursday via overnight mail, so at least he had something to show the people who came!

Be prepared and be flexible. If your book is going to be effective in winning ground for Jesus and taking back ground from the enemy, you will experience opposition. If it can go wrong, it will. So think ahead and don't plan things too close to the publication date.

A very helpful resource for the marketing process is *1001 Ways to Market Your Book* by John Kremer. This book's 500 pages contain great ideas and suggestions; it retails for $19.95 in most secular bookstores. Even though it is geared to the secular market, you will still glean some great information.

Now it's time to move into the nitty-gritty details of producing a quality product. If you're like most people, you'll want to delegate this end of the publishing process to a professional. But whether you do it all yourself or farm the work out, you still need to be informed of how the pieces of the book production puzzle fit together.

Eight

Producing a Quality Product

ASSUMING THAT YOU have *already* spent the time, money, and effort to have your manuscript edited and fine-tuned, you are ready to begin the production process. When you get to this point, you want to be sure your manuscript is at least 99 percent complete. If you decide to add a chapter or rewrite a section of the book once the editing and typesetting have been completed, not only will you waste precious time, but you will incur additional charges because the production work will have to be redone. There are many good books out that cover all the details of prepress and actual printing; it's not my purpose to repeat that information here. My goal is to simplify the process so that you can understand the steps and the importance of each one.

COVER
Everyone judges a book, at least to some degree, by its cover. The cover is not only there to package and protect what is inside, it is also your best advertising. Your cover will either sell your book or kill sales. It must be quality work that communicates your point effectively and persuades the potential reader to pick up the book.

The front cover draws interest, but once the customer has it in his hands, what happens? You guessed it! He turns the book over and reads the back cover to see what it is all about. If this piques his interest, he may scan the table of contents. That's why it's crucial not to skimp on your cover. You may think you can only afford a two-color cover; but believe me, the money you spend to ensure that your cover is professional, eye-catching, and powerful will be money well spent. I recommend a four-color cover by a professional artist or graphic designer.

When WinePress first began publishing, I thought our covers looked 200 percent better than most self-published books, but I still knew they did not look like the "real thing" on the shelves of Christian bookstores. Even though bookstores are not generally outlets for large independent sales, I still wanted to see our authors' books looking just as good as the "big guys." So, just like we recommend you do, we invested in a very talented, full-time graphic designer who makes our authors' work look first-class.

No matter how you publish, whether on your own or with a book packager, be sure to have a professional-looking cover printed on 10-point stock with UV-gloss lamination applied. This will give your book the look and feel of strength and character. You may even want to spend a bit more and add some special options to your cover, like foil embossing the title and combining matte and high-gloss lamination. This is what you see on the cover of this revised and expanded edition of *You Can Do It!* Again, people do judge a book by its cover, so don't skimp!

TEXT PAGES

Your next choice will be what kind of text paper you will use. The paper available falls into the following three basic categories.

1. NEWSPRINT OR GROUNDWOOD PAPER. This paper is very inexpensive and tends to yellow within a few years. Some high-end groundwood does allow for good photo

reproductions, but the low-end paper does not. If you have a long manuscript and need to cut costs in every way possible, you may want to consider using this type of paper to bring the cost down.

2. UNCOATED BOOK STOCK. This is your typical 50- to 60-pound, white or cream colored paper. This is the most common stock used in books. Your photos will reproduce well.

3. COATED BOOK STOCK (MATTE, COATED, OR GLOSS). This kind of paper is great for gift books, photo inserts, and four-color printing; but as you can imagine, it's quite expensive. For most books, the text pages are printed in one color: black. If you have a special project that requires more than one color on the text pages, you can expect to pay quite a bit more.

Now for the *look* of the text pages. Some people tell me their book is "camera ready" and they want a quote on printing only. Then, when they send me their manuscript for review, the page layout is set two-up with no crop marks—in Courier type. This is hardly considered camera ready, although there are some in this industry who would have no problem printing that for you. Not only does the publisher look bad in such an instance, but so do *you*.

Because there are so many variables, it's well worth enlisting the services of professional editors and typesetters to clean up and format your manuscript. But the following are some basic guidelines that will help anyone improve a cluttered page.

1. Indents at the beginning of a paragraph should be 0.25 inches. Use the tab key to indent; do not use the space bar.

2. Use only one space between sentences instead of two.

3. Be sure to use typographers' quotation marks and apostrophes (" " & ' '), not the marks for inches and feet (" & ').

4. Learn the difference between hyphens (-), en dashes (–), and em dashes (—). Use them correctly.
5. Use a traditional or classic-looking font for your text, such as Berkeley, Garamond, Caslon, Palatino, or Century. Using common fonts (Courier, Times New Roman, Arial, or Helvetica) or trendy design fonts will make your work appear less professional. Scan through some of the books on your shelf from Thomas Nelson, Word, or Bethany House; you'll see the difference.
6. Be consistent with the layout of chapter titles, subtitles, subheads, running heads, etc.

Fᴏɴᴛ Sɪᴢᴇ ᴀɴᴅ Sᴘᴀᴄɪɴɢ

The easiest type size to read is 12-point type with 14.4-point *line spacing* (also called *leading*). Smaller type and line spacing are possible, but the text becomes more difficult to read. If your software supports *tracking* (adjustable space between the letters), you'll want to be sure that it is set on "Normal." A setting of "Loose" or "None" will cause the word and letter spacing to look inconsistent.

Qᴜᴏᴛᴀᴛɪᴏɴᴜ ᴀɴᴅ Sᴄʀɪᴘᴛᴜʀᴇ Rᴇᴠᴇʀᴇɴᴄᴇᴛ

Be sure to quote Scripture accurately. Nothing ruins your credibility more than sloppy quotations. Short quotations of a verse or two are customarily placed within the running text in roman type. The proper punctuation can vary depending on the sentence structure, but a common quotation might look like this: "The tongue of the wise uses knowledge rightly, but the mouth of fools pours forth foolishness" (Prov. 15:2). Notice that the closing quotation marks are at the end of the scripture, there is one space before the reference, and the period is outside the closing parenthesis.

Block quotations are large portions of text set off from the running text. Indent both margins an additional one-quarter inch, insert one space above and below, and drop the font size one point. After the closing punctuation add the reference in parentheses only. Here is an example of a short block quotation:

> And when it was evening, there came a rich man from Arimathea, named Joseph, who himself had also become a disciple of Jesus. This man went to Pilate and asked for the body of Jesus. (Matt. 27:57–58)

Also, you must list on the copyright page of your book the version of the Bible you quoted. If you are using more than one version, you must give credit to those additional versions. One way is with a notation at the end of the reference: (Matt. 27:57–58, NKJV). If you quote extensive portions of Scripture, you may have to pay a fee to the publisher of that translation. In most cases it is considered *fair use* to quote from a book as long as the proper credit is given.

The following questions and answers from Woody Young's *A Business Guide to Copyright Law* will help you determine whether or not you need to obtain permission.

> **Q:** How do you determine what constitutes fair use? Am I safe to assume that I can quote up to 250 words without getting permission?
> **A:** When it comes to fair use, you can assume nothing. Although the law defines fair use it is not a black and white issue. Most questions fall into a gray area. The law gives no specific number of words that can safely be quoted without permission. . . . Use your common sense. If the quote is of a minor nature, such as one anecdote from a whole book, you will probably not need to ask permission. However, if you take the [ten] steps to a happy marriage, on which the book is based, you are taking the heart of that author's material and would be infringing on his copyright. The only rule is: When in doubt, ask.[1]

CHAPTERS

Ideally, all chapters should start on odd-numbered pages—as you open a book, they should always be on the right-hand side. Depending on where each chapter ends, you may end up with a blank left-hand page every so often. This is not a problem, unless you are trying to cut every corner. While the professional style of having all chapters start consistently on a right-hand page is nice, it is not absolutely necessary. If you are planning a 144-page book and the right-hand style has caused you to be two or three pages over, you can probably get back on target by starting the chapters on both the odd- and even-numbered pages.

HEADERS AND FOOTERS

Running heads are usually placed at the top of a page to inform the reader of her present location within the book. You'll want your *verso* (left) running heads to display the title of the book and the even page numbers. The *recto* (right) running heads should display the chapter title and the odd page numbers. Or, page numbers (*folios*) may be placed at the center bottom of the page in an invisible box known as a *footer*, or at the upper or lower outside margin—wherever you or your designer think best.

FOOTNOTES AND ENDNOTES

Whether you use footnotes or endnotes depends on several factors: content, length, book dimensions, and style preference. If your text includes footnotes and it's not absolutely necessary that the reader survey that information immediately, I would encourage you to create an endnote section and place it after the epilogue and before the bibliography. The notes will be much easier for you to format, and the reader will have all the notes in a tight package.

PAGE COUNT AND MARGINS

Here's a helpful formula to use to estimate page count: Every double-spaced manuscript page in 12-point type (250–300 words) will produce roughly one published page in 12-point type with 14.4-point leading. So, if you have 100 double-spaced manuscript pages in 12-point type with standard margins, you'll end up with a 96-page book. If you have

100 single-spaced manuscript pages, you'll have a 192-page book.

Most printers we work with use a 32-page signature. The book is printed on large sheets of paper, such as 24" x 36", and folded down and trimmed to make 32 pages that measure 6" x 9" or so. If your book lays out at 102 pages, you will either have to get it down to 96 or go up half a signature (16 pages) to 112. For camera-ready pages, set your margins at 0.75 inches on all sides; on a custom 6" x 9" page, you will end up with a text block measuring 4.5 inches wide and 7.5 inches from top to bottom.

WIDOWS AND ORPHANS

If you're creating camera-ready text pages, you'll need to set your software to catch all the *widows* and *orphans*. A widow is the first line of a paragraph that appears by itself at the bottom of a page. An orphan is the last line of a paragraph that appears by itself at the top of a page. You should never have fewer than two lines of running text starting or ending a page. Eliminating these will be an additional way to guarantee that your text looks clean and professional.

PHOTOS AND ILLUSTRATIONS

Many people like to include photographs to give the reader an example from the story or visually bring some of the characters alive. While photos aren't found in most books on the Christian bookstore shelves, they are quite common in self-published books.

You will end up paying anywhere from $10 to $30 for each photograph you have *halftoned*, captioned, and stripped into your manuscript. (*Halftoning,* or *screening,* is a process that turns the photograph into a mass of dots that pick up ink during printing.) If you are creating your own halftones on the computer, be sure that you check with your print shop to find out what *line screen* to set. Usually a line screen of 150 is adequate. Photos should be sized to fit into the text block set for the page.

Also, you have the choice of placing your photos through-out the text, at the end of the book, or directly in the center. Some people even like to print their photos on glossy text stock that can be inserted as its own section. This, of course, is more costly, but it ensures higher quality photo reproduction.

BINDING

You have several choices when it comes to binding. The most common for a standard, trade-size, softcover book is *perfect* binding—a squared-off spine on which the title and name of the author may be printed. In order to have a perfect-bound book, you generally must have a minimum of forty-eight pages.

I have noticed that there are different qualities of perfect binding. I am frequently disturbed at the stiffness of the perfect binding and the general feel of some printers' samples. Many just feel cheap. A quality, perfect-bound book should be flexible, and the pages should fall open easily. The book should not snap shut, and the binding should not crack when you open up the book too far. Be sure to ask your printer or book packager for some samples of their work so you can see the quality of the binding.

Some types of perfect binding have the *lay-flat* feature, useful for cookbooks and workbooks. This helps a book to open flat. It is much better than comb or spiral binding because you still have a spine available on which to print the title and the author's name. If your book is ever carried in a bookstore, it is imperative that the spine be easy to read. That tiny width may be all the advertising space you get.

For books under forty-eight pages, or for some workbook formats, *saddle-stitch* binding is inexpensive and appropriate. The book is stapled or wire-stitched on the fold in the center.

The last type of binding I'll suggest for a softcover book is called *spiral wire*. This type of binding allows workbooks, manuals, and cookbooks to have the "lay-flat" feature, but at a higher cost since the process is very labor intensive.

Your alternative to softcover is a *casebound* or hardcover book. While this generally costs about $2.50 to $3.00 more per book to manufacture, you are able to charge an extra $6 to $8 to the customer. The additional revenue looks great on paper, but there is always the possibility of losing sales on a book that retails for $15 to $25. Some people won't buy a book if it costs that much, but there are others who prefer hardcover books.

REGISTRATION AND COPYRIGHT

If you are determined to undertake the whole publishing project by yourself rather than having a professional do it for you, the best place to get all the forms necessary (i.e., to purchase an ISBN, Library of Congress number, copyright, bar code, etc.) is from Dan Poynter's Para Publishing. Poynter's *Secret List of Book Promotion Contacts* gives you everything you'll need. While most of the information in Poynter's book *The Self-Publishing Manual* relates to the secular media and publishing industry, it does have all the information you'll need to learn how to register your work.

BOOK PRODUCTION SEQUENCE

1. COMPLETE THE MANUSCRIPT. Read your manuscript one more time. You don't want to rewrite in the middle of production. Enlist the services of an experienced editor or professional critique service to help you direct the rewriting process. They can help you define your audience, focus on that audience, and keep that audience hungry for future books. If you are working with a book packager, they will most likely have these additional editorial services available.

2. DETERMINE YOUR BEST PUBLISHING ROUTE. Do it all yourself, farm out various tasks to different resources (cover designer, editor, typesetter, etc.), or farm out the entire project to a reliable book packager or consultant.

3. REGISTRATION BEGINS. Apply for an ISBN and Library of Congress number. Generate a bar code for the cover.

4. COVER DESIGN. Since you'll be using the cover for your promotional material, it is good to get this going early. Typically a designer or book packager will take your ideas and add their expertise to make it look professional. You will need to give your designer a photograph of yourself for the back of the book and determine how the cover copy is going to read. Some book packagers and consultants will take care of writing the copy for you after you give them an idea of what you want to accomplish.

Once the page count is confirmed by the typesetter, the spine width can be calculated and included in the design. After the final revisions, the designer sends the file to a service bureau or prepress house; there the final film is created. A high-resolution proof from them will ensure that the film is going to reproduce the way you expect.

5. FORMATTING AND TYPESETTING. Begin while the cover is being designed. Typically you will submit your manuscript on disk to your typesetter or book packager. You will also give them a *hard-copy* printout.

If you have entered your entire manuscript on an outdated word processor and your files are not compatible with today's computer formats, you will need to have those files converted.

If your manuscript was typed on a typewriter and is not available in any electronic format, you will need to have it rekeyed in the proper format. The other option is to have the pages *scanned* into the computer. Depending on how clean the pages are, scanning may be less expensive; but you'll have extra proofreading to do because some scanning software misreads certain characters.

If you are including photos, illustrations, or charts, the typesetter will need them on disk or as halftoned/camera-ready art for placement in the layout. If you do not have them camera ready or on disk, your typesetter can have this done for you, but they will probably charge a service fee.

Normally you will see two sets of *page proofs*. These are your manuscript pages laid out with crop marks on 8.5-x-11-inch paper. The crop marks indicate where the pages will be trimmed. Read the page proofs over carefully to be sure everything is correct. As I mentioned earlier, this is not the time to start adding a lot of material or doing rewrites. Doing so at this stage of the game will only rack up a hefty bill on top of the typesetting quote you already received.

6. BLUELINES. Once you have approved the second set of page proofs and the cover film has been created, you are ready to go to press. When the text pages arrive at the printer, they are photographed. From that film the printer produces *bluelines*. This is your last chance to ensure that everything is in the right place. You can make changes at this point, but, as always, it costs money when the printer has to process film. Some printers charge anywhere from $7 to $20 per page to process film, so be careful! Do your eagle-eye proofing on the second set of page proofs—don't wait for the bluelines.

Once you return the bluelines with your approval, the text pages and the cover are printed separately. Then they are bound and trimmed, usually in-house. The next thing you see is your baby—your book! It will have been a long pregnancy and sometimes a confusing and emotional labor, but when you are holding your book in your hands, all those anxieties and frustrations slip away. Your baby has been born.

Remember, however, your "baby" needs to be shared with the world, so marketing your book is the next step to consider.

Nine

HOW TO MARKET
YOUR BOOK

W HEN YOU PROMOTE your book you are not promoting
yourself, you are promoting the *message* God has given
you!" These wise words were spoken by an author friend of
mine not long ago, and they have influenced my perspective
on writing and publishing.

Many people say they feel funny about promoting their
own book—they think it's prideful and pushy. I felt the same
way when my first book came out, until my friend spoke those
words. All of a sudden I was boldly talking about my book,
and you should too. If the Lord has given you a message to
communicate, you needn't be shy about it. He wants you to
get it to the people who need to hear it. The Lord's plan for
your life and your book probably does not include a long-
term lease on a dusty storage space.

DEVELOP A MARKETING STRATEGY

When you begin to think about your marketing plan, you
need to ask yourself these questions: What problem am I solv-
ing with the message in my book? Who needs to hear my
message? Where can I find these people? How can I let them
know about my book? With the answers to these questions
you should be able to effectively formulate your strategy.

There are four basic ways to let people know about your book.

1. MEDIA EXPOSURE: radio, TV, and print interviews; excerpts, articles, and reviews.
2. ADVERTISING: in-trade publications; distributors; catalogs, magazines, and niche newspapers; the Internet; through direct mailings.
3. IN-PERSON PROMOTION: speaking engagements, book readings, and autograph parties.
4. TRADE SHOWS: setting up a booth at a trade show or convention, such as CBA, NRB, etc.

We'll talk more about the different venues for promotion in the next chapter, but first let's be sure you have the proper tools to present your product.

CREATE MARKETING TOOLS THAT STAND OUT

Let's face it, people are drawn to color. If all your marketing tools are created in black and white or one-color ink, their impact will be greatly diminished. That's why we always use the *four-color process* (full color) for our marketing tools.

Some of the most popular ways we've found to promote books are with the following four items. Sample prices are included for comparison, but prices are subject to change.

1. FOUR-COLOR POSTCARDS (3.5 by 5.5 inches).

500	$.50 each
1,000	$.27 each
2,500	$.14 each
5,000	$.08 each

2. FOUR-COLOR BOOKMARKS (2 by 5⅜ inches). They are a great way to promote your book. Readers love free bookmarks, and it's good advertising.

500	$.41 each
1,000	$.23 each
2,500	$.11 each
5,000	$.065 each

3. FOUR-COLOR BUSINESS CARDS (2 by 3.5 inches; four-color on one side, black text on back). Some authors will put their book cover on the full-color side and their name and ordering information on the other side. Pass them out everywhere.

1,000	$.20 each
2,500	$.10 each
5,000	$.06 each

4. FOUR-COLOR SALES FLIERS (8.5 by 11 inches; four-color, one side). Design and film not included in these prices.

1,250	$235.00
2,500	$285.00
5,000	$390.00

Keep in mind that before your flier is printed you'll have to pay for flier design and film. Feel free to do your own homework, but unless you have an uncle who is a printer, you'll be hard pressed to find rates this low at a local print shop. In fact, every time I compare, local printing rates are usually two to three times higher than these numbers. Appendix 1 has a list of vendors with great printing rates.

PUBLICITY KITS

At WinePress we design high-end, full-color publicity kits for our authors. But you could just as easily create one yourself. Our kits start with a textured presentation folder and a color copy of the book's cover on the front.

For the contents we use a high quality paper stock to complement the front-cover colors. We then create a one-page summary of the author, a second page that describes the book, a third page that includes endorsements and positive comments, and a fourth page of suggested interview questions.

For marketing purposes we create a full-color sales flier that shows the cover of the book and gives all the primary information on one page: subject overview, selected endorsements, ordering information, etc. We also include a set of full-color postcards. Each kit is a polished and professional representation of an author, helping to build credibility and a great first impression with industry representatives.

Tabletop Displays and Signs

You can find a great variety of various tabletop displays that will give your book table a professional look. Also, if you have the potential of securing a booth at a trade show, which will attract your buying public, you may want to invest in a trade-show-style tabletop display.

Now that you understand the importance of looking sharp, it's time to get your book out there so the world can see and hear the message God has given you.

Ten

CREATING A DEMAND FOR YOUR BOOK

IF YOU HAVE A MESSAGE that people need to hear, then, with the Lord's help and direction, you need to create a demand for your book. You need to expose your message to as many different markets as possible, in as many different ways as possible. I can't say enough about developing a speaking ministry—if you have that gift and it is confirmed that the Lord wants you to do it.

If you feel you need some training in this area, I can recommend Christian Leaders, Authors & Speakers Services (CLASS). Their seminars are presented in major locations across the country by Florence and Fred Littauer, organized by their daughter Marita. CLASS seminars are usually in a three-day intense format. You might also consider joining a local Toastmasters group to polish your public speaking skills.

One example of creating demand through a speaking ministry is from a 1994 *Writer's Digest* article:

> When a computer search at my library revealed almost no books on how to develop a close grandparent/grandchild relationship, I decided to self-publish my first book, *Grandparents' Little Dividends: How to Keep in Touch*. I genuinely wanted to develop, in book form, my ideas on

how to close the gap [with] my own seven grandchildren, particularly with the four that lived a considerable distance away from me. I also wanted to use the book in classes I'd be teaching in the fall. I knew that looking for a publisher was going to take time, more than I was willing to wait. I didn't even try to find a publisher. Here's how I went about the project.

First, I increased my visibility and credibility as a grandparent expert. I led seminars on grandparenting at local community centers, taught classes at local colleges, spoke to grandparents at retirement centers, churches, temples and corporations. In short, I created valid credentials. I reached the point where the *Kansas City Star* dubbed me the "guru of grandparenting" in a feature article.

I spent six months collecting information on creative ways to make the grandparent/grandchild connection. I gave out surveys and networked with grandparent groups around the country.

Nine months later, the writing of my book was completed, and I joined a critique group. I took a few worthwhile suggestions and made my revisions. . . . In 1989, I published my first 2,000 books at a production cost of $3.50 per book. The softcover book sold for $8 per copy. In less than one year, and with no advertising, I had sold all but 100 books.[1]

My point in sharing that story is to illustrate the power of building a platform in the public speaking arena. This author found that selling her book was easy because of her visibility at many speaking engagements.

The following are some other avenues for creating a demand that you should prayerfully consider. Contact information is listed in appendix 1.

1. CHURCH LIBRARIANS. The best way to reach them is to have your book reviewed in *Church Libraries* (formerly *Librarians World*), a publication of the Evangelical Church Library Association (ECLA). I would also suggest that you place an ad in the issue in which your book review will be seen.

2. CHRISTIAN SCHOOL LIBRARIANS. If your book is appropriate for Christian school libraries, you will want to have *The Christian Library Journal* review your book. This publication is distributed to a large number of Christian school librarians, and it also accepts advertising.

3. MINISTRIES AND NONPROFIT ORGANIZATIONS. Do your homework and see if there are ministries or nonprofit organizations that might be interested in offering your book as a *premium* (fund-raiser giveaway). Depending on your topic, your local church may even be able to use it as a fund-raiser for missions, youth, or other departments. You would have to give them a 50 to 60 percent discount, but you would be selling books by the case.

4. MAGAZINE SUBSCRIBERS. We had a new author whose book was not scheduled to be out until late October, but he thought ahead and got information on advertising in *New Man Magazine* for the November/December issue. Since his book, *Why Christian Men Don't Date*, is a humorous look at the issue, he knew that it would be worth targeting that market for Christmas sales.

   If your advertising budget allows, one great way of reaching a specific audience is to query the magazine about using an excerpt—possibly allowing you to write the article—or having them write a book review. If any of these possibilities materialize, consider buying an ad in that issue. This can be a risk, however, since you have no guarantee of sales.

5. CHRISTIAN RADIO OR TV AUDIENCES. Your best shot at these markets is to launch a media blitz through a reputable Christian publicist. You must be a great communicator to be successful in this area. If your tendency is to speak in a monotone without much "pizzazz," then you'll probably be wasting your time and money trying this approach.

There is a new program on the market offered by Advocate Media out of Chesapeake, Virginia. They have a team of highly professional media experts (many of whom formerly produced *The 700 Club*) who have created a promotional package to help self-published authors get the exposure they need. You'll notice that I have listed them as a resource in appendix 1.

6. SECULAR RADIO OR TV AUDIENCES. If your book is geared to the secular market, is not overtly Christian (i.e., quoting Scripture and using Christian jargon), and you are an effective communicator, your best way to get booked on secular radio and TV is through *Radio-TV Interview Report*. This magazine is read by all the talk-show hosts and producers. It can really generate interest. The advertising is not overly expensive, and for the right topic, this can be an effective way to reach the masses with your message.

7. THE SECULAR LIBRARY MARKET. The best way to reach this market is through Quality Books, a distributor to both public and school libraries. Though they buy your books on consignment at a steep discount, this is still a great way to get into that market.

8. ONLINE SERVICES/INTERNET. The effectiveness of this has not yet been accurately measured, but there are some possibilities. However, unless you are selling a get-rich-quick guide that tells how to make money on the Internet, the chances are slim that you'll recoup all of the expense of creating a Web page on your own and/or buying advertising space on the Internet.

To help authors minimize the financial risk of testing these new waters, we have begun to include in our standard publishing package an automatic listing in our WinePress Online Bookstore catalog. It includes a dedicated Web page, full-color cover sample, book overview, author contact information, and an online order form. Visitors to our Web page can download the catalog, but sales vary with trends and the effectiveness of other marketing strategies.

One other nifty idea that doesn't cost much money is an online service like America Online (AOL). You can find the *message boards* of people who would most likely be interested in your book.

One area of AOL where this has been successful is Christianity Online. I found an area for pastoral research, posted messages about our publishing services, and began to get many responses. The key is to come up with the right wording for the subject line of your message. If the subject doesn't catch someone's eye, he or she will never bother to click on your item to read what's in the body of the message. My subject line read: "You Can Publish Your Book." When people opened the message they read our story of self-publishing *Nam Vet*. They could then respond for more information.

We also found a whole section where Vietnam veterans would "hang out" online. So we also posted information there about the *Nam Vet* book. Our subject line for that read: "The Solution for PTSD!" Not only did we sell some books, but some of those guys got saved!

9. NARROWLY TARGETED MAILING LISTS. There are a few Christian companies that specialize in selling the mailing lists of churches, ministries, people who have purchased a product out of XYZ Christian magazine, people who subscribe to XYZ Christian magazine, and so on. If you can narrow your target market to a category listed in one demographic base, you won't waste money mailing advertisements to people who haven't historically been interested in your topic.

10. CHRISTIAN BOOKSTORES VIA DISTRIBUTORS. Not the easiest market to tap, but with the right message, packaging, and marketing plan, it is possible.

11. CATALOGS FOR CHRISTIAN BOOKSTORE CUSTOMERS. If you have a highly marketable product and a hefty advertising budget, you may want to consider buying a spot in some catalogs. Your ad could cost anywhere from $3,000 (Family Bookstores) to $1,800 (The Munce

Buying Group) to $1,000 (Your Stores chain of 200 Christian bookstores). The nice thing about buying into a catalog is guaranteed sales. The bookstores that distribute the catalog ensure that they have stock on hand for all the products in the catalog. But again, it is not easy to get in. Your book has to really look good, and it has to *be* good. Many of the catalogs have committees to decide which titles should be accepted. From the limited tests I have done in this area, I'm not totally convinced that this is the best route for the money.

Now it's time for the distribution end of things. Let's see how we can get your well-marketed book to your waiting customer in the quickest, most professional manner.

Eleven

MAKING YOUR BOOK AVAILABLE

O NE OF THE BIGGEST challenges for the self-published author is figuring out how to make his or her book available to those who need to read it. If you think that most people are going to take the time to write out a check, lick a stamp, address an envelope, and run up to the mailbox in order to get your book, you need to wake up and smell the coffee! Most people today want to be able to do one of two things to get their hands on a Christian book: call a toll-free number to order it with a credit card, or stop by their favorite Christian bookstore to pick it up.

It is wise to be extra efficient at making your book easy for people to obtain. If you're only planning to market at your speaking engagements, at meetings of organizations, or to the people you see on a daily basis, then this isn't a big issue. As long as you have books, people can purchase them easily. But those of you who are seeking a wider audience or national recognition need to prayerfully consider the following proven ways of making your books obtainable by the greater public.

CHRISTIAN BOOKSTORES

While the national market is getting harder and harder to break, you may do well with your local Christian bookstores. Some may be willing to purchase small quantities of your book for a 40 to 45 percent discount. Others may take them on consignment. Unfortunately, since larger corporations are buying up many of the small Christian bookstores, buyers are no longer employed at the store. Purchasing is normally done in large quantities, at large discounts, directly from the big publishers and distributors.

CHRISTIAN BOOK DISTRIBUTORS

I just can't stress this enough: Don't get your hopes up on this one! The Christian bookstore market is so competitive that your book must have national appeal (i.e., no poetry, missionary stories, or general testimonies—unless you are famous). Your book must also be extremely well written and have sufficient dollars behind it to support large advertising and media campaigns. Since most Christian book distributors won't even look at your book if they know that you're self-published and not an established author, chances are slim.

Again, through test marketing and promoting my own book, I've found ways around this avenue that can be beneficial to some WinePress authors.

FULFILLMENT

The best way to make your book easily available to the general public is through a *fulfillment* service. This gives customers a toll-free number they can call to order your book with their credit card. The service includes warehousing the inventory, answering the phone, taking orders, and shipping the product. The average amount you'll pay for this kind of service is 35 to 50 percent of the retail price of the book. You can organize this service yourself, if you really want the hassle.

For my first printing of *Consumed by Success*, I fulfilled my orders through a secular company named Bookmasters. When all was said and done, I paid just over 50 percent of the book price for that service. They charged me for every little thing, including warehousing, insurance, inquiry calls (which do not necessarily turn into orders), charge-card fees, order fees, administrative fees, and so on. They are, however, a very reputable company, and I felt the service was a valuable one. When I did the *Prime Time America* show with Jim Warren on the Moody Network, we gave out the toll-free number and sold over 700 copies of my book in an afternoon. So it was important to have a company that could handle that kind of volume. I was certainly glad to have someone else taking those calls and handling the orders!

As you research fulfillment services, be sure to ask how many operators they have on duty around the clock. Some have only a few people answering the phones. If you land a syndicated radio interview, your service might not be able to handle all the calls. Every lost call is a lost sale. Also, be sure to request a statement of charges ahead of time to learn what will be covered.

I finally became so discouraged with what was available out there that I established a fulfillment service for WinePress authors. We keep it simple: Don't nickel and dime people to death. And since it's not our main source of income, we are able to keep the cost down to a reasonable amount. Recently we transferred our answering service to the same company that handles all the calls generated by the *Insight for Living* radio broadcast. Because this is an all-Christian company, I know that our potential customers will not only be taken care of professionally, they'll be treated like a Christian, by a Christian. Also, now we have the increased capacity we need, so when a WinePress author makes his or her debut on *Focus on the Family* or some other large radio ministry program, we are able to handle all the calls.

Our most recent success story happened when Dan Miller appeared on the *Hour of Power* show with Dr. Robert Schuller. He did a twenty-minute interview, and Dr. Schuller gave out our 800-917-BOOK number about ten times during the interview. Within four days we had about 2,500 orders for Dan's book, *Living, Laughing and Loving Life!* Even with the 30 percent fulfillment charge, the income he generated from that one show actually paid for the entire print run of 10,000 books.

Book Table

During speaking engagements, your book table at the back of the room is your primary means for making books available. Be sure the table looks good, with professionally produced signs and a handsome display of your books. You can usually find inexpensive, tabletop plate holders at craft shops to display your book in a way that looks sharp. Be prepared with lots of change, and keep several pens handy— people will often ask you to sign your book.

Order Information

Place your ordering information on the first available right-hand page that follows the last text or reference section of your book. Confused? See our order page at the end of this book.

And be sure to check out the laws in your state. Most states require that you establish a business license and a *resale account* with the Department of Revenue, since you are purchasing your books at a wholesale price and reselling them at a retail price. When you sell to someone who lives in your state, you usually have to charge them the appropriate sales tax. Presently you don't have to charge sales tax when you sell to someone who is out of state. The simplest way to handle the bookkeeping is to keep track of the amount you take in for sales tax and set it aside in a savings account. Then, once a quarter or once a year when you have to fill out the paperwork to pay your sales taxes, you've got the money in hand.

Now that your book is well marketed and distributed, let's make sure we make the most of the media.

Twelve

GETTING THE MOST OUT OF THE MEDIA

IN PREVIOUS CHAPTERS I've emphasized the use of the media to help generate exposure for your book. My good friend and publicist Don Otis, from Creative Resources, has given me permission to edit and reprint some incredibly detailed and important publicity how-to information he has compiled but never published.

Part I: Getting Started
Language and Words: Using Words Effectively to
Communicate Your Message

The goal of communication is to impart what you know or believe to your audience. This means selecting the words you use very carefully. Jesus used stories, parables, and allegories to communicate in ways that His hearers could understand. The words you choose can be powerful. They can also be dangerous. The art of using words to persuade is called *rhetoric*. This is a basic part of scholarly discipline. It is also necessary if you want to communicate your message. By using words in certain ways, we can manipulate people to do just about anything. Hitler is proof enough. His two most potent weapons were sloganeering and repetition.

Author Steve Brown says, "The goal of communication is not to impress, but to communicate clearly." And a major element of clear communication is simplicity. Cleverly chosen language has the effect of simplifying ideas rather than complicating them. Intellectualizing often confuses the listener instead of imparting ideas, concepts, or information. As writer E. B. White said, "Avoid the elaborate, the pretentious, the coy, and the cute."

Language has been called the greatest drug known to humanity. Jesus said [that our words justify or condemn us] (Matt. 12:37). The way we use words, and how we define them, has an effect not just on what we think but on how we think. Politicians, social engineers, and the military are clever in cloaking the true meaning of their words in euphemisms. They obscure realities we'd rather not deal with. For example, "collateral damage" refers to civilian casualties. When the military "redeploys troops," it often means retreat. Our prison system uses "honor ranches" in place of prisons and "boys' homes" rather than juvenile detention. Each of these [is an] example of hiding the truth with words.

Words are powerful. They are so powerful that God confused languages to control the effect words had on the human race. [Words] put into languages are the most complex creation of the human mind. Babel is testament to the creative power and influence of words. God used words to create the world and all that it contains (Ps. 33:6). By our words we can create and build. And by our words we can dismantle or inflict pain. It is not by accident that the countries with the most advanced technology also have the fewest languages. And the world's 6,000 languages are gradually disappearing. This global language extinction is leading us back to the place where communication was first scrambled in Babel.

EXPECTATIONS

Working with a publicist will help you get the most out of your publishing experience. Even before your book is off the press, the work to promote it has begun. Once it is off the press, promotion moves into a more aggressive mode. Publicists view the promotion of your book as a joint venture. By this I mean a positive author-publicity relationship will ensure that your book gets the best media coverage. Your participation in the media and promotion process will directly influence the sales and success of your book.

Here is what you can expect from a good publicist.

They will . . .

- Write and prepare press materials. These are written to attract the attention of a host or producer. They do not try to portray every major aspect of your book.
- Prepare questions for your interviews.
- Mail information about your book to appropriate media sources.
- Provide a review copy of your book to interested media.
- Work with you to schedule media opportunities.
- Send review copies of your book to book reviewers.
- Send review copies to key influencers and opinion makers.
- Provide "coaching" help for interviews.

Publicists do not . . .

- Handle the shipping or mailing of your books for special meetings or events.
- Serve as a public speaking agency.
- Place space ads in magazines or newspapers.

PUBLICITY: WHAT IS IT?

We define publicity broadly to mean "any reasonable opportunity to gain public exposure for an author to promote their product." The idea is to attract public interest in your book. A good publicist focuses most [available] resources in three main areas: radio, television, and print media.

Radio

There are more than 1,300 Christian radio stations scattered throughout the United States. Christian radio now represents the nation's third largest format. Many of these stations have regional talk shows. A good publicist will use whatever creative means available to position you for an appearance on these regional or national programs. It is a publicist's job to secure airtime for you. It is your job to promote your book or product. Most radio talk programs fall into issue-related classifications like family, theology, politics, or current events.

Let's take a brief look at some characteristics of radio interviews. Your interviews will last between 15 minutes and one hour. Most interviews can be done by phone from your home or office. Radio interviews will be either taped or live. When your publicist confirms an interview with you, the form will tell you which it is.

- Radio is fast moving. Be prepared to respond as quickly as possible to questions.
- Some live radio programs will open phone lines for callers.
- Radio is personal. Though many people are listening at any given time, you are being heard by one person at a time. Individuals are listening in their cars, on the job, or at home.
- Radio is an effective tool for communicating your message.
- Some radio hosts will be excited [by] or sympathetic with your topic. Others may disagree or sound disinterested.

Here are a few items to remember when you're doing an interview:

- Be enthusiastic. Be positive and energetic.
- Be relational. Try to identify with the host or the city you are being heard in.
- Use short examples, stories, or research findings to bolster your main points.

- Keep a marked-up copy of your book close by. Flag the pages you might quote from.
- Be on time.
- Be prepared. If you use notes, keep them close by. For call-in programs, we suggest you keep a notepad nearby. Write down the names of callers so you can respond to them by name.
- Keep a glass of water nearby.
- If you are doing a phone interview, be sure to eliminate any distractions ahead of time. Find a quiet place away from children or noise. If you have call waiting on your phone, have it turned off during your interviews.
- Listen to the questions carefully and respond appropriately and you'll do fine.
- Be timely. If your book or product can be tied to a particular current event, use it.
- Be courteous to the host and callers.
- Be gracious. Be sure [to] thank the host for having you on.

Now that we've covered what you should do, let's look at what you should avoid during a radio interview.

- Avoid euphemisms. This is a Greek word meaning "using auspicious words." Make yourself understandable to as many people as possible.
- Avoid using legal terms (unless you explain what they mean and they are relevant to the interview).
- Avoid theological terms (same rule applies).
- Avoid medical or psychological terms.
- Don't insult your host either directly or indirectly.
- Do not assume people know what you're talking about. No one knows your book (or subject) as well as you. Your tendency will be to assume that the people listening know more than they do. A word of caution: Be careful not to patronize or talk down to the host of audience just because you do know more.

- Don't use clichés.
- Avoid name dropping.
- Do not embellish or exaggerate.
- Avoid gossip or talking down about others.
- Be careful not to "over promote" yourself. Some hosts will cut you off immediately if they feel you're using their show as an extended commercial.

Television

There are fewer than 200 Christian television programs in the United States. While most of these are regional, some are national like *The 700 Club*. Television is also distinctive because it engages several senses at the same time. Television is also very different from radio because you have to be there to do the interview. That's why it's important that you let your publicist know about any travel plans you may have as far in advance of a trip as possible. Sometimes your publicist can schedule you on television during your travel.

Here are some things to remember when doing television interviews:

- Avoid bright colors, especially white.
- Respond to the host rather than looking toward the camera.
- Arrive early for television tapings.
- Don't take notes with you.
- Bring at least one or two copies of your book with you.
- Bring a set of questions.
- Body language is important on TV. Don't slouch or fidget. Never assume the camera is *not* on you.

Print

Books, newspapers, and magazines are the primary print media. The print media fall into several classifications: Christian tabloids, Christian magazines, secular newspapers and magazines, and ministry newsletters or magazines. In each case, remember who you are talking to. Be relevant. If you do an interview with a secular publication, learn as much as you can beforehand about the person who is interviewing you. Try to find out the angle they are looking for. What can you find out about their own beliefs? How will they use [them]? Have they interviewed anyone else on the subject? Use words sparingly and use them carefully when talking with secular journalists.

Usually your publicist works to obtain book reviews on every title they represent. This does not mean that every book will be reviewed in major publications. However, some local secular newspapers and Christian newspapers will review your book. Sometimes when review copies of your book are sent out, a publication will decide to run an excerpt. If you have contacts with either local Christian or secular print media, let your publicist know. [Your publicist] will work with your local newspapers.

Publicity: What You Can Do

Typically, authors believe their job is over when their book goes to press. As mentioned before, promotion is a team effort. Even during the height of a publicity campaign there are things you can do to provide an extra publicity boost.

- Always carry a couple copies of your book with you. If you travel, keep one in your car or carry-on bags.
- Introduce yourself to local bookstore owners or buyers. If they are not carrying your book, ask them to.
- Ask your friends or family living in different areas to call their local bookstores and ask them to carry your book.
- If you do public speaking, be sure to have plenty of copies of your book on hand for your meetings. Most churches will provide someone to handle a book table for you. If you're invited to speak at a church meeting or seminar, ask the host to provide a table. When speaking publicly, be sure to mention the availability of your book.

Part Two: The Interview Process
Working with Your Publicist: Getting the Most Out of Your Media Campaign

What is a media campaign? Most would define a campaign as a four- to six-month effort to provide the greatest possible media exposure for your book. Here are a few quick tips to help you work effectively with your publicist.

- Provide a travel itinerary.
- Provide a list of the best or worst times for doing interviews.
- Respond quickly. An interview can be lost when an author takes too much time to respond to an interview opportunity. If you are exceptionally busy, provide your publicist with "the holes in your schedule" and they'll do their best to work with you. If you have done interviews before, let them know about it. It is easier to go back to "good interviewers" and avoid those [who] were unpleasant. If you have contacts with any media, let your publicist know about them.
- If you have specific questions you want to be asked about your book, be sure to let your publicist know before they put your prepared questions together.
- They can do a better job for you if you take the time to let them know your ideas up front.

A Typical Interview: What Can I Expect?
If you've never done a media interview before, don't worry. Just remember, you're the expert! After you've done several interviews you will find yourself repeating many of the same things. You will also discover there are good and bad interviewers. The best interviews are those where the person who interviews you has actually read your book. However, sometimes you will find hosts who have just skimmed your materials. Once in a while, you will find yourself in an interview with a host who hardly remembers your name! If this happens, take control of the interview by discussing your book or topic. In many instances,

this will bring relief to a host and salvage an otherwise wasted interview.

A typical interview includes at least three sections: an opening (this is where having a good bio is important), the body of the interview (the content), and the close (the wrap-up). If you are on a live call-in program, a fourth ingredient will include the callers.

The opening is important since it sets the stage for both the host and the listeners (or viewers). The introduction establishes your credibility to say what you have to say. If this is done ineffectively, you can recall your credentials without sounding arrogant. For example, "While I was conducting my research at Harvard, I discovered . . ." Or, "When I studied law the two things I found most disturbing were . . ." If a host has your biography and does [his or her] job well, you can stick to the subject.

The body of the interview will generally follow [one of] two directions: [The interviewer will] use the prepared questions or [he or she will] use a more spontaneous approach. A good host will gently challenge your assumptions by asking questions anyone in the audience would ask if they were there. Don't be offended by the "devil's advocate" questions. These do not necessarily mean a host disagrees with you.

The close of the interview should consist of a brief recap of what your book is about. It must also include a mention of the book and where listeners can get a copy. . . . [T]he onus is on you, not the host. If the book has not been mentioned, you might ask (on the air), "May I mention where your listeners (viewers) can find my book?" If you have time before the interview, ask the host if you can mention where to find the book.

A final word about the interview process. You will find some radio interviews are on commercial stations and some are on [noncommercial] stations. On commercial stations you can expect frequent interruptions (every 7 to 12 minutes) for a commercial break. Use this time to gather your thoughts and prepare for the next segment. Interviews on [noncommercial] stations will generally have few if any interruptions.

Preparing for an Interview: What You Should Know

There is an English proverb that says, "Hope for the best, but prepare for the worst." Just like any other job, interviewers have good days and bad days. If you happen to hit one on a bad day, try to make the best of your time. And just as interviewers have bad days, so do authors. Authors don't do interviews for a living, so the likelihood of something going wrong is even greater. This shouldn't scare you but it should keep you on your toes. The best interviews are with authors who are rested and alert. Your interview will be as successful as you are prepared—mentally and spiritually.

What to avoid during an interview

The best advice I can offer is to "be yourself." Be who you are without any pretense. Be natural and relaxed. Too much anxiety will rob you of your ability to think clearly. However, having said this, a little fear can also be a good thing. It is also very normal. Author Steve Brown calls fear "a wonderful motivator." It can be an encouragement to keep you mentally alert.

Here are some tips to help you relax:

- Imagine that you are talking with only one person.
- Take a deep breath before you go on the air and during any commercial breaks.
- Take a moment to pray before you go on the air. If you can, pray with the host; this is even better.
- Know your material. You are at an advantage because it is your material you're discussing. Don't be led into discussions on topics you don't know anything about. If you are an expert on "home schooling," don't be pulled into a discussion about "How to discipline children." If you find yourself "off track," don't be afraid to say something like, "I'm sure there are better qualified people to discuss that subject, but I can tell you more about . . ." This can get you and the host back on track and away from things that are unconnected to your book.

- Finally, don't act bored by the interview. If you're bored, chances are good that the audience and host will also be bored. Enthusiasm can make even the most trivial conversations seem more interesting. Frank Sinatra once said to his son, "Don't ever let me catch you singing like that again, without enthusiasm. You're nothing if you're not excited about what you're doing."

What to remember during an interview

The most important thing to remember is that you don't have to be perfect to be effective. Keep your answers simple. Keep them short. Remember that your job is to hook the listener so that he will want to know more about what you have to say. You don't have to cover everything in your book in a thirty-minute interview. That's not possible anyway. If you feel pressed for time, you can say, "I cover this issue more fully in chapter 7 of my book. . . ."

The beginning of your interview is like the beginning of a speech. Your audience will make a quick judgement about whether they want to listen to you. Your opening comments will set the stage for anything else you have to say. In his book *How to Talk So People Will Listen* (Baker Books), Steve Brown offers the following do's and don'ts for speeches. They are equally applicable for media interviews.

- Don't apologize. Do not say, "I haven't done very many interviews before so I'm rather nervous." If you are doing an interview by phone, just pretend you're having a normal conversation with a friend.
- Don't demean. The audience is giving you their time. You owe them something. Don't insult them.
- Don't patronize. The audience will tune you out if you come across as arrogant.
- Do get the listener's attention. Start by citing something to perk the audience's attention. This can include a piece of research, a quote, or simply an enticing opening comment.

- Do whet the listener's appetite. Asking the listeners a question is a good way to keep them thinking. You can "bait" and keep an audience by saying something like, "I'll explain this in further detail later, but first . . ."
- Do give the listeners your theme. Be sure you state and restate what your book is about. Ask yourself, "Why would a person want to hear what I have to say?"

Afterward: What to do when you hang up the phone
Some authors actually take notes during an interview. This makes sense if you want to remember names or keep on track during the interview. [They are] also very helpful to use . . . if you write the interviewer a note of thanks. Most of us are like the nine lepers who after they were healed by Jesus went on their way. Set yourself apart by sending a brief note of thanks to the interviewer. The form your publicist sends you to notify you [about] your interview will have the name and address of the person you do [the] interview with.

Part III: Interview Tactics and Questions
How to Promote Your Book without Sounding
Like a Commercial

Many of us have difficulty promoting ourselves. That's normal. The trick is to find ways that accomplish your purpose (promoting your book) without sounding like an infomercial. It's actually much easier than you might think.

If you do an adequate job of creating an appetite for your book, the host will be more assertive in asking you where your book can be purchased. The better you are at tantalizing the listeners, the greater the motivation to buy your book. For example, let's say you have a book called *Seven Godly Principles to a More Fulfilling Marriage*. If you simply give all these principles away during an interview, the listener has no need to buy your book. A smart way to create interest is with a comment or phrase. Using the example above, you might say something like, "My fifth principle has to do with sex, but it's not what you think." This statement creates more curiosity or a desire to know more.

The most difficult thing most authors face is how to promote their book during an interview. The interview itself should take care of this dilemma. As you are asked specific questions, answer them succinctly without going into too much detail. Use the end of your comment to say something like "I wish we had time to go into further detail on this, but if you'd like more information on this you can find it in chapter 3 of my book." This does not sound overly promotional but does leave the listener with the idea that he is far better off to get the book if he wants to know more.

Depending on the availability of your book, you'll want to encourage listeners to call your 800 number rather than going to their local bookstore to purchase your book.

DIPLOMACY: HOW TO HANDLE TRICKY QUESTIONS

There are several useful rules for handling tricky or difficult questions during an interview. If you remember these rules, you can get out of almost any tough situation.

- RULE #1: You don't have to answer every question. This may sound odd if you're doing an interview. However, there will be some questions that are not relevant to your book. If they are "out of bounds," don't be afraid to say so. For example, "I wish I had an answer to that question myself!"
- RULE #2: You are not an expert on everything. Isn't that a relief? If you don't have an answer, don't pretend you do. There is nothing wrong with saying "I don't know." You will get into far more trouble trying to answer questions you know nothing about.
- RULE #3: Don't argue with the host. This does not mean you can't disagree. The key word here is argue. This will quickly destroy an interview. How do you avoid arguments? One of the simplest ways is to ignore statements you might otherwise feel

compelled to correct. If it is important, disagree with it. If you do, be willing to cite your reasons, research, or sources. Remember the old adage, "The customer is always right." The same rule applies to interviews, unless the host is stealing your wallet!

- RULE #4: Diversion is the best method to avoid confrontation. If you are asked a question you don't want to answer, then answer something else. What do you do if the host asks you, "Have you beaten your wife lately?"

   Since no answer is a good answer, you might respond by saying, "That's a good question, but what my book is really about is how to minimize the effects of violence in the family."

LIVE SHOWS: WHAT TO DO WITH ANNOYING CALLERS

The job of the producer is to screen callers. The job of a good host is to keep the interview from getting off track. It's their job to control the interview. Callers often have their "own agenda." If the host doesn't keep things on track, then don't be afraid to do it yourself. A caller may ask, "Do you believe that UFOs are sent from the devil?" If your subject is about marriage, you might say, "I have no idea, but I would be glad to answer any questions about marriage."

There are different types of callers. They are lonely, argumentative, fixated [on some subject other than yours!], and those who really are interested. You never know for sure which one you'll have until they're on the line. But that's what makes talk-radio so interesting. You must immediately assess which category the caller falls into. If someone wants to argue, don't argue back. Try to be soft and gentle without compromising your position. The key is to pacify the caller. When you use an angry caller's first name, [that] can [work] wonders to soothe his anger. For example, "Steve, that's your name, isn't it? I know you're frustrated by what I've said, but please try to see it from a different perspective." In almost every instance you can win the heart of a caller by identifying with them in some way. This is not just clever manipulation but show[s] genuine interest in them or the difficulty they're facing.

FIVE QUESTIONS AUTHORS ASK MOST

1. Do interviews really sell books? The answer is yes. [They are] second only to public endorsements from others or your own meetings.
2. How many interviews will I do? The answer to this question depends upon the subject of your book. The range of interviews is anywhere from [twenty] to [seventy] interviews, with [thirty] to [thirty-five] being about average.
3. What if I need to cancel an interview? If you cannot do an interview that has already been scheduled, call your publicist right away. Don't wait until the last minute.
4. Can I get a copy of my interview? In most cases the answer is yes. Let the host know in advance that you want a copy of the interview. If you are doing a television taping, take an extra video cassette along with you.
5. When will I be on *Focus on the Family, The 700 Club* or *Oprah?* The larger the program the harder it is to schedule an interview. For example, *The 700 Club* receives 300 to 400 program suggestions every week. With only five or ten guest openings per week, they schedule between [1] and [3] percent of the program ideas they receive.

Part IV: Speaking from Experience
What Makes a Good Interview: A Host's Perspective

"I look for someone who can bring a biblical perspective to an issue. I want them to focus on a real life issue."
—*Bill Feltner, KNIS Radio*

"An author needs to be able to express the essence of their book. I like an author who will deliberately connect with me as a person."
—*Ron Reed, Lifetime Radio*

"The author should always be more prepared for an interview because there is no guarantee the host will grasp all the content. Always provide a solid, firm answer to a question. Keep it simple for the audience. Remember that your personality is a turn on or turn off to the listener."

—John Young, WNIV Radio

SOME FINAL ADVICE FROM TALK-SHOW HOSTS

- Send a thank-you note.
- Don't assume the audience knows who you are. Most people have probably never heard about you before.
- Don't overpromote your book.
- Every interview is a new interview. If you act disinterested, it will turn off the audience.
- Ask for a cassette copy of your interview and then critique it. Ask yourself, "Would I listen to myself?"
- Make sure the audience knows your name. If they can't remember the title of your book, they may remember your name.
- Make sure the listener knows how to get a copy of your book.

Well, now that we've covered all your options, let's get to the resources so you can start planning your project and get things underway.

EPILOGUE

I HOPE THIS BOOK has encouraged you to move ahead with the publishing of the message God has given you. I hope it has been informative, helpful, and interesting to read. It has been my prayer that *You Can Do It!* would benefit Christian writers. I want to inform you of all of your options and give you the tools and knowledge you'll need to undertake whatever portion of the publishing process that you decide to tackle.

This book is meant to augment other more detailed books on self-publishing and to amplify the specifics as they relate to the Christian market. While many of the other books I have recommended are excellent, they still cite secular resources for advertising, distribution, and other facets of publishing. This normally won't do you any good if you've written a book with an overtly Christian message. Thus the need for information geared to the Christian writer. In sharing this information my hope is that you have gained the confidence to *do it!*

I'd like to close with the following quotation, which was forwarded from the Internet. The author is unknown, but I am sure it will encourage you to keep on keepin' on!

YOUR WORK

The Lord has given to every man his work. It is his business to do it—and the devil's business to hinder him if he can. So, sure as God has given you a work to do, Satan will try to hinder you. He may present other things more promising, he may allure you by worldly prospects, he may assault you with slander, torment you with false accusations, set you to work defending your character, employ pious persons to lie about you, editors to assail you, and excellent men to slander you. You may have Pilate, Herod, Annas, and Caiaphas all combined against you, and Judas standing by ready to sell you for thirty pieces of silver. You may wonder why all these things come upon you. Can you not see that the whole thing is brought about through the craft of the devil to draw you off from your work and hinder your obedience to God?

Keep about your work. Do not flinch because the lion roars; do not stop to stone the devil's dogs; do not fool away your time chasing the devil's rabbits. Do your work. Let liars lie, let sectarians quarrel, let corporations resolve, let editors publish, let the devil do his worst; but, see to it that nothing hinders you from fulfilling the work that God has given you.

He has not sent you to make money. He has not commanded you to get rich. He has never bidden you to defend your character. He has not set you at work to contradict falsehoods that Satan and his servants may start to peddle. If you do these things, you will do nothing else; you will be at work for yourself and not for the Lord.

Keep about your work. Let your aim be as steady as a star. Let the world brawl and bubble. You may be assaulted, wronged, insulted, slandered, wounded, and rejected; you may be abused by foes, forsaken by friends, and despised and rejected of men; but see to it with steadfast determination, with unfaltering zeal, that you pursue the great purpose of your life and the object of your being until at last you can say, "I have finished the work which Thou gavest me to do." Amen.

Appendix One: Resources

Advertising Contacts

Christian Library Journal, The
   Nancy Hesch, Editor
   801 S. Osage Avenue
   Bartlesville, OK 74003-4946
   (918) 336-0813

Church Libraries
   Lin Johnson, Editor
   PO Box 353
   Glen Ellyn, IL 60138
   (847) 296-3964

Book Distributors

Appalachian Distributors
   PO Box 1573 (522 Princeton Road)
   Johnson City, TN 37601
   (800) BUY-APPA

Dick Sleeper Distribution
(represents small-press authors)
18680-B Langensand Road
Sandy, OR 97055-9427
PH: (503) 668-3454
FX: (503) 668-5314

Ingram/Spring Arbor Book Distributors
One Ingram Boulevard
La Vergne, TN 37086-1986
(615) 793-5000

Quality Books, Inc.
(secular libraries)
1003 W. Pines Road
Oregon, IL 61061
(815) 732-4450

Riverside Book & Bible Distributing
636 S. Oak (1500 Riverside Dr. is warehouse)
Iowa Falls, IA 50126-0370
(515) 648-4271

Successful Living Book Distribution
4050 Lee Vance View
Colorado Springs, CO 80918-3665
(719) 535-0318

Whitaker Distributors
30 Hunt Valley Circle
New Kensington, PA 15068
(412) 274-4440

BOOK PACKAGERS/CONSULTANTS

I am only comfortable recommending companies that do quality work and have a track record of integrity. So, while this list does not include all the Christian companies that are available, these are some that I can personally endorse. Although there may be other organizations that do equally fine work, I know these people and am well acquainted with their staff, their work, and their commitment to biblical values.

ACW Press, Steve Laube
5501 N. 7th Avenue, Suite 502
Phoenix, AZ 85013
(800) 931-BOOK

Fame Publishing, Maggie Kinney
820 S. MacArthur Boulevard, Suite 105-220
Coppell, TX 75019
(972) 393-1467

Longwood Communications, Murray Fisher
397 Kingslake Drive
DeBary, FL 32713
(904) 774-1991

WinePress Publishing, Chuck and Athena Dean
PO Box 1406 (12108 Mukilteo Speedway)
Mukilteo, WA 98275
PH: (800) 326-4674
FX: (425) 353-4402
EMAIL: Publish4U@aol.com
HOME PAGE: http://www.winepresspub.com

FOUR-COLOR PRODUCTS AND DISPLAYS

Avery Color Studio
(800) 722-9925
3,000 full-color, high-gloss postcards (3.5" x 5.5") $397

Coru Displays
(tabletop and freestanding displays)
1450 Park Court
Chanhassen, MN 55317
(800) 430-6111

Mitchell Graphics
    2363 Mitchell Park Drive
    Petoskey, MI 49770
    (800) 583-9401
    1,000 full-color cards (4" x 6") $199

Paper Direct
    (800) A-PAPERS (for a catalog)

Traverse Bay Display Company
    (countertop book displays)
    (800) 240-9802

Tu-Vets Corporation
    5635 E. Beverly Boulevard
    Los Angeles, CA 90022
    (213) 723-4569
    Four-color, one side (8.5" x 11"); no design included
    in these prices

Fulfillment Companies

The Vantage Group
    1830 Air Lane Dr.

1,250	$235.00
2,500	$285.00
5,000	$390.00
10,000	$600.00
20,000	$1,070.00

    Nashville, TN 37201
    (800) 699-9911

WinePress Publishing
    (fulfillment for WinePress authors only)
    PO Box 1406
    Mukilteo, WA 98275
    PH: (800) 326-4674
    FX: (425) 353-4402

MAILING LIST COMPANIES

Doug Ross Communications
  1969 E. Broadway Road, Suite 4
  Tempe, AZ 85282
  (602) 966-1744

Response Unlimited
  c/o The Old Plantation
  Rt. 5, Box 251
  Waynesboro, VA 22980-9111
  (540) 943-6721

Williams Direct
  PO Box 205
  Burlington, KS 66839-0205
  (316) 364-8431

PUBLICISTS AND PROMOTION

Advocate Media Group
  908 Ventures Way, #9
  Chesapeake, VA 23320
  (888) 863-2988

CLASS Promotional Services, Kim Garrison
  5201 Via Pauma
  Oceanside, CA 92057-4526
  (760) 630-2677

Creative Resources, Don Otis
  PO Box 1665
  Sandpoint, ID 83864
  (208) 263-8055

International Media Services, Dorothy Miller
PO Box 1800
Hemet, CA 92546
(888) 925-6460

Jakasa Promotions, Jacqueline Cromartie
108 Fairview Parkway
Lafayette, LA 70508
(318) 981-6179

National Religious Broadcasters (re: directory)
7839 Ashton Avenue
Manassas, VA 20109
(703) 330-7000

Radio and TV (secular)

Radio-TV Interview Report
Jack Lewis
Bradley Media Publications
135 E. Plumstead Avenue
Lansdowne, PA 19050-8206
(610) 259-1070

Suggested Reading

Christian Writers' Market Guide, Sally Stuart (Wheaton, IL: Harold Shaw Publishers, 1998).

1001 Ways to Market Your Book, John Kremer (Fairfield, IA: Open Horizons, 1993).

APPENDIX TWO:
BUDGET

PRODUCTION COSTS

Quantity _____ x $_____ per book = $_____
Shipping $_____
Overrun (10% max.) $_____

Marketing Materials
1. Four-color postcards ($.08–$.50 each) $_____
2. Postcard postage ($.20 each) $_____
3. Mailing list price ($60–$75 per 1,000) $_____
4. Bookmarks ($.07–$.40 each) $_____
5. Media blitz (with publicist: $400/mo. for $_____
   4–6 mo.)
6. Cooperative advertising ($150–$400 per $_____
   quarter)
7. Additional publicity kits/promo $_____
8. CBA exposure/personality booth $_____

Miscellaneous Marketing Expenses
1. Telephone $_____
2. Postage $_____
3. Travel/CBA/events $_____

TOTAL COST $_____

BALANCE

Books sold to break even _____ $_____

(Total cost ÷ retail price = books sold to break even)

POTENTIAL PROFIT

Balance of books _____ x $_____ = $_____

ENDNOTES

Chapter 1

[1] "Downsizing Hits Thomas Nelson," *Publisher's Weekly*, (October 16, 1995), 11.

[2] *Writers Information Network Newsletter*, (February–March, 1996), 4.

[3] *The Written Word*, WinePress Publishing, (vol. 1, no. 1, Summer 1995), 6–7.

[4] "Whatever Happened to Christian Publishing?" Gene Edward Veith, *World*, (July 12/19, 1997), 13–15.

[5] "Not-by-the-Books," *U.S. News & World Report*, (vol. 112, no. 22, June 8, 1992), 73.

[6] *The Self-Publishing Manual*, Dan Poynter (Santa Barbara, CA: Para Publishing, 9th ed., 1996), 25–28.

[7] *Is There a Book Inside of You?* Dan Poynter and Mindy Bingham (Santa Barbara, CA: Para Publishing, 4th ed., 1997), 26–27.

Chapter 2

[1] "Self-Publishing Successes," *Publisher's Weekly*, (May 22, 1995), 23.

Chapter 4

[1] *The Self-Publishing Manual*, 16, 19, 22–25.

[2] An excerpt from a letter dated February 28, 1996, from the acquisitions editor, Bridge-Logos Publishers.

Chapter 5

[1] All commercial printing has a 10 percent margin that is legally bill-able to the client. This means you could end up with 10 percent more than you originally ordered, and you are expected to pay a lower rate for those additional books. If the printer prints more than 10 percent over, the additional copies are yours at no charge. This is a standard in the industry and is unavoidable.

Chapter 8

[1] *A Business Guide to Copyright Law*, Woody Young (San Juan Capistrano, CA: Joy Publishing, 1988), 22.

Chapter 10

[1] "Self-Publishing Technique," *The Writer's Digest* (vol. 74, no. 11, November 1994), 36.

To order additional copies of

YOU CAN
Do It!

send $9.99* plus $3.95 shipping and handling to:

Books, Etc.
PO Box 1406
Mukilteo, WA 98275

or have your credit card ready and call:

(800) 917-BOOK

*Quantity discounts available